THE INSIDER'S GUIDE TO SPECIAL EDUCATION ADVOCACY

TAKING THE PATH TOWARD SUCCESSFUL IEP & 504 ADVOCACY

"The primary responsibility of an effective parent-advocate is to move the process from emotionally charged conversation to an evidence-driven approach. By shifting the dialog from subjective to objective reasoning, you will gain control of your child's education plan, and in the process, empower the team to co-create the best IEP/504 plan possible for your son or daughter."

Larry Martin Davis

"If we all did the things we are capable of doing, we would literally astound ourselves." - *Thomas Alva Edison*

Table of Contents

Introduction: (*For 1st Time Advocates or a Refresher Course for Experienced Advocates*)

Before the Meeting: Do Your Homework *(For Experienced & 1st Time Advocates)*

During the Meeting:

After the Meeting: Following Through

Introduction:

For most parents, the education advocacy path may be one of the most difficult challenges one faces, for it can be emotionally draining and a potentially frustrating process. Thank you for reaching out, and opening yourself to the possibility of being the best parent advocate for your child. This valuable handbook provides "insider" guidance; whether you are navigating the special needs process through an IEP or a 504 Plan with little or no experience; or you are a parent familiar with special education and the school system. These effective strategies will streamline your efforts toward successful advocacy, empower you through information, and minimize the level of aggravation you may experience. As a result, you will increase your ability to <u>take control</u> of your child's educational plan through an easy to follow process from an "insiders" perspective. I am confident, if you follow this handbook from cover to cover, you will be an extraordinary parent advocate!

The "Insider's Guide" provides a step by step method for you to follow, as you embrace your role as your child's advocate in IEP or 504 meetings. Whether you are addressing disabilities such as ADD/ADHD, Autism, neurological disorders, or specific learning disabilities found within reading, writing, math, or communication, effective advocacy skills significantly impact your child's success at school. Developing the best educational plan will require you to be informed and prepared beyond what you may be comfortable with, especially if you go it alone without the essential advocacy tools. For this reason, the "Insider's Guide" is written for you; providing you with a parent friendly advocacy tool kit!

Since I began negotiating IEP and 504 Plans as an Education Advocate in 1998, and in my former role as a school administrator facilitating IEP <u>and</u> Section 504 meetings, I learned the need to disengage oneself emotionally from the advocacy process, and take an objective perspective. As a parent advocate, it can be a challenge to remain neutral during the process, for the conversations focus on your child; the love of your life. The strategies prescribed within the "Insider's Guide" will help develop your focus, create a well-thought approach, and most important, empower you to take charge of your child's educational plan, in contrast to the emotional roller coaster often associated with the special needs path. The primary responsibility of an effective advocate is to move the process from an emotionally charged conversation to an evidence-based decision process when working with teachers and staff. By shifting the dialog from subjective reasoning to objective understanding through a strategic, evidence-driven approach, you will take control of your child's IEP or 504 Plan process!

Rather than feeling upset, confused, withdrawn, or distraught by the uphill battle often experienced by parents with special needs children, you will feel informed and empowered as you follow the guide. Specifically, the purpose of this guide is to share what I successfully do as an experienced Education Advocate so you can strategically co-create the best IEP/504 plan possible for your child! The path to successful parent-guided advocacy is based upon the following guidelines which will be explained more within this handbook:

Ten Commandments of Parent Advocacy:

1. Know about your child from a "school perspective" and establish yourself as the most informed member of the team related to your child strengths, talents, and challenges; do your homework!

2. Establish "mutual understanding" across the table as you move through the IEP or 504 intervention process, guided by the following fundamental questions:

    a.   Is there a disability or diagnosis identified by clinicians or medical professionals?

    b.   How does this disability or diagnosis impact my son or daughter's school experience including academic, social, emotional, or behavior considerations?

    c.   Finally, how will Specially Designed Instruction through an IEP or General Education accommodations (Section 504 Plan) best support my child?

3. Never detour from your set intention no matter what comes back at you; stay the course!

4. Acknowledge your child's strengths <u>and</u> disability through mutual understanding first and foremost; moving into quick-fix solutions without fundamental understanding may later prove to create a weak platform for intervention like a house built of straw.

5. Create an in-depth understanding through a well-defined "Present Levels of Performance"; establish an evidence-based snap shot of your child from a well-rounded perspective at home and at school: ❑ Academic ❑ Behavior ❑ Cognitive ❑ Communication ❑ Emotional ❑ Physical ❑ Social

6. Establish related Accommodations (504), and if needed, Specially Designed Instruction (IEP), guided by your child's formal Evaluation from outside of the school conducted by clinicians, physicians, and specialists, as well as the internal school-based evaluations; don't follow personal experience alone.

7. Always stick to the facts and hold on tight when the pressure gets intense, don't fold. Take your time and allow the school-based evidence, data, and test information guide your course of direction rather than emotions, frustration, and lack of patience, possibly expressed by you or staff members.

8. Write everything down and keep a record of what is said at all times, as if you are preparing to go in front of a Due Process judge or an investigative agency. (Though, you won't likely do so!)

9. Ask questions when you are uncertain of what is being discussed or decided. Remember you always have options including: *Procedural Safeguards:*

    ✓ <u>Independent Education Evaluation</u>: an outside evaluation if you need more information.

    ✓ <u>Mediation</u>: a neutral non-binding problem solving process conducted by a facilitator.

    ✓ <u>Due Process Hearing</u>: a binding decision process conducted by a neutral judge.

    ✓ <u>Citizens Complaint</u>: a formal investigative process guided by education agencies.

10. Seek guidance of professionals who have walked this path, when you feel you have hit the wall [i.e.; Advocates, Attorneys, and Ombudsmen]. Their experience and wisdom can be priceless!

Information is Everything!

When looking to make a major purchase, like a new car, one might assume sales people may take advantage of a person's lack of inside information about the auto industry and the buying and selling process. As a result, savvy consumers utilize resources like Kelly's Blue Book, Consumers Guide, and other tools to level the playing field, because knowledge is power. Knowledge is also your best tool as a parent advocate within the complex systems of school districts and working with special education personnel. Assuming the school system is set-up to "do what's best for my child" is misleading. Keep in mind: IEP and 504 plan development requires parents to negotiate like any other important business transaction; requiring a level-head, a significant amount of "homework" in preparation for the meetings, and confidence before going to the table and negotiating on your child's behalf.

It is important to understand that the notion schools are run by shady teachers and administrators is also far from the truth. Teachers, staff, and administrators are genuinely caring individuals; working with significant resource limitations. Often they feel pressured to resolve learning challenges with district "best practices" and one-size-fits-all formulas, and meeting compliance guidelines. As a result, your child may not receive essential services due to the nature of a bureaucratic process. District policy often creates quick-fix solutions to very complex kids and the challenges each presents within the context of "square pegs fitting within a round holes".

The purpose of the "Insider's Guide" is to arm you with information, strategies, and insights supporting your advocacy efforts. Your role as parent-advocate is to assure your child has a successful learning experience in school, supported by a balanced approach of accommodations and individualized planning. This is in contrast to your child needing to exclusively fit-in whatever the cost. As advocates, we are trying to minimize this experience by creating mutual understanding across the table between parents and staff, and at the same time, maximize creativity, innovation, and collaboration.

As long as you go-it-alone as your child's advocate, you need to be well informed and ready to present a compelling case in light of your child's challenges, talents, and special needs and the significant impact each has on his/her success at school. Again, stay the course, connect the dots between your child's disability and his/her "present levels of performance", and guide the process from subjective to objective reasoning, founded upon mutual understanding. It's time for you to do your homework!

Key Words and Phrases to Know: *Just Enough to be Dangerous!*

FAPE: The Section 504 regulation requires a school district to provide a "free appropriate public education" (FAPE) to each qualified person with a disability who is in the school district's jurisdiction, regardless of the nature or severity of the person's disability.

IDEA: The Individuals with Disabilities Education Act (IDEA) is a law ensuring services to children with disabilities throughout the nation. IDEA governs how states and public agencies provide early intervention, special education and related services to more than 6.5 million eligible infants, toddlers, children and youth with disabilities.

<u>DECISION MAKING</u>: Ideally, the process should be collaborative and supports genuine partnership.

Consensus: Group decision-making process in which group members develop, and agree to support a decision in the best interest of the whole.

Mutual Understanding: A relation of affinity or harmony between people; whatever affects one correspondingly affects the other; all for one and one for all!

Evidence-Based Decision: Evolved from medical culture, and emphasizes a rational, objective, and empirical – data approach to addressing issues and decisions.

<u>INTERVENTION</u>: When students are not succeeding or meeting standards, supports are developed.

Response to Intervention: A multi-tier approach to the early identification and support of students with learning and behavior needs. The RTI process begins with general education Instruction and universal screening of all children.

Title I Support: Educational supports provided by the federal government for disadvantaged students requiring intervention in critical learning areas; an extension of general education.

Functional Behavior Assessment (FBA): A behavioral assessment is generally a problem-solving process for addressing student behavior. The process relies on a variety of techniques and strategies to identify the purposes of specific behavior and to help teams select interventions to directly address the problem behavior. In theory, the team is trying to understand the purpose of the behavior and follow up with interventions which would increase positive behavior and diminish disruption.

Section 504 Plan: Educational support provided for identified disabled students through accommodations within the general education program; requires an annual review.

IEP and Specially Designed Instruction: Specially designed instruction for identified students provided by district special education services following a formal evaluation process; highlighted by an individual education plan (IEP).

Present Levels of Performance: Current state of a student's progress highlighted by evidence, assessments, and observations.

Goals: Specific learning targets based upon the identified areas requiring specially designed instruction: "moving from [point a] … to [point b] … as measured by …"

Service Matrix: identifies the services, related support, and the minutes provided in support of the specially designed instruction.

ESY: additional services over the summer in situations where extraordinary regression or loss of skills would take place during the break.

<u>EVALUATION</u>: Formal process usually conducted by a School Psychologist to explore potential disabilities and its impact on learning; outside evaluations may be utilized within this process.

Discrepancy Model: A comparison between <u>ability</u> based upon IQ scores and <u>achievement</u> as measured by various assessment tests; typically using standard scores between 90-110 as the "average" range.

Specific Learning Disability: (may include, but not limited by the following)

Reading Comprehension: The ability read text, process, and understand its meaning.

Reading Fluency: The speed in which one reads text.

Reading Symbol Recognition: The ability to interpret reading letters and symbols.

Math Computation: The ability to apply basic functions; add, subtract, divide, multiply.

Math Problem Solving: The ability to utilize computation within real applications.

Written Expression: The ability to write down information and ideas (using sentences, paragraphs, correct grammar and spelling) such that the intent of the author is clear and can be understood by others. It is a complex process that involves organization, structuring sentences, correct grammar and correct spelling.

Health Impairment: According to IDEA, Other Health Impairment is defined as: having limited strength, vitality or alertness, including a heightened alertness to environmental stimuli, that results in limited alertness with respect to the educational environment, that is due to chronic or acute health problems such as asthma, attention deficit disorder or attention deficit hyperactivity disorder, diabetes, epilepsy, a heart condition, hemophilia, lead poisoning, leukemia, nephritis, rheumatic fever, and sickle cell anemia; and adversely affects a child's educational performance.

Executive Functioning: Executive Functioning (and self-regulation) are the mental processes that enable us to plan, focus attention, remember instructions, and juggle multiple tasks successfully. ADD/ADHD as well as Autism diagnoses present organization and planning challenges associated with EF.

PROCEDURAL SAFEGUARDS: Dispute resolution resources available to parents guided by state and federal laws including:

Mediation: A process facilitated by a neutral, non-bias, third party when both parents and school districts agree to work toward a collaborative resolution.

Independent Education Evaluation: An outside evaluation, paid for by the district, provided to the parents, when the district-developed Evaluation is in question.

Citizens Complaint: A formal complaint based upon IDEA/FAPE guidelines presented by parents or other informed parties; typically presented to the state or regional offices.

Due Process: Either the parent/adult student or the school district has the right to request a due process hearing whenever there is a dispute between the parent and the school district over the district's proposal or refusal to initiate or change the identification, evaluation, proposed IEP or portion thereof, the implementation of the IEP, educational placement, or the provision of a free appropriate public education (FAPE). Simply, it's when a resolution case goes before a judge.

Manifestation Hearing: When a child with an identified disability, supported through a 504 or an IEP, engages in behavior or breaks a school code of conduct and the school proposes to remove the child, the school must hold a hearing to determine if the child's behavior was caused by his disability. This hearing, known as a Manifestation Hearing, is a process to review the relationship between the child's disability and the behavior, guided by the evidence presented.

The Squeaky Wheel Gets the Grease:

Before you picked up the "Insider's Guide" you already suspected or knew that your son or daughter faced challenges at school as a result of an impairment, disabling condition, or you felt "something was just not right". Also, we all want the very best for our children and sometimes we fear placing a negative spotlight on our child by "labeling them" _different_. As a result, it is a natural reaction to let things slide and hope they will "grow out of it". For children with special needs, this is often not the case: things can get worse over time, especially when dealing with neurological conditions such as ADD/ADHD, Autism/Asperger Syndrome, Anxiety Disorders, and Learning Disabilities in reading, math, writing, or communication.

Yes, your child is different! Everyone is. Also, she/he is a gift to the world. However, in many situations, it _will_ require a well-designed advocacy plan to help the school system see your precious "diamond in the rough" as you do, and design a specific education plan with their amazing gifts and strengths in mind.

Here are the facts: There are a significant number of children facing similar challenges in the school system as your son or daughter. In many communities, 20% or more of the school-age children are diagnosed with ADD or related attention developmental disabilities. Also, we read about Autism and an epidemic level of kids found to be on the spectrum. In many schools, over 20% of the student body have an established IEP or 504 Plan addressing disabilities, creating a never-ending challenge for our schools today. At the same time, while increasing numbers of children are identified with special needs, the financial resources are not keeping up with the growing numbers of identified students. This creates a tendency for the schools to work within a one-size-fits-all set of strategies, resources, and accommodations for these kids. Like most other customer service industries, "the squeaky wheel gets the grease". This is no different within the context of public education.

No matter what image the local media, elected politicians, and teacher unions represent: schools are _not_ able to meet the needs of _all_ students; test scores and graduation rates clearly point this out. On the other hand, if you want to hear about excellent customer service in the schools, ask parents who volunteer endless hours, such as the PTA President, how well he or she is treated at his/her school. You will hear nothing except accolades and commendations, for extraordinary service requires extraordinary effort! It's a numbers game for the squeaky wheel gets the grease within an overwhelmed school system. Certainly, not everyone can be the PTA President nor volunteer thousands of hours. So it's paramount that you "squeak" with knowledge and authority. By doing your homework and following this handbook, you will be impressive as you present yourself as your child's best advocate.

IEP and 504 Plan Basics:

When addressing special needs and related disabilities, specifically, disabling conditions which have a significant impact on learning, schools utilize two programs: Special Education through the IEP (Individual Education Plan) process or General Education accommodations addressed within Section 504 Plans.

When comparing the programs, the decision process guiding the two is founded upon the same three leading questions:

1. **Is there a disability or diagnosis identified by clinicians or licensed medical professionals?**

2. **How does this disability or diagnosis impact my son or daughter's school experience including academic, social, emotional, or behavior considerations?**

3. **Finally, how will Specially Designed Instruction through an IEP or General Education accommodations (Section 504 Plan) best support my child?**

Breaking it down further, the difference between the two programs is based upon the severity of the "substantial limitation" demonstrated by the disability and diagnosis. Whereas, the accommodations and resources established, in support of your child's academic needs, will determine if intervention is founded by a 504 Plan or an IEP. However, the three guiding questions, proposed earlier, serve as the foundation for both:

An IEP requires <u>specially designed instruction</u> and additional support typically outside of the general education classroom program (sometimes through "inclusion" practices in the class.) These additional services require funding above and beyond what the basic general education provides including: Instructional Assistants supporting instruction in the classroom, resource teachers instructing smaller groups, or specialists required to administer therapies like speech and language, and costly assistive technology support. Here are a list of possible services supported by an IEP:

- Academic support
- Audiology services
- Counseling services
- Early identification and assessment of disabilities in children
- Medical services
- Occupational therapy
- Orientation and mobility services
- Parent counseling and training
- Physical therapy
- Psychological services
- Recreation
- Rehabilitation counseling services
- School health services
- Social work services in schools
- Speech-language pathology services
- Transportation

The Section 504 Plan supports accommodations handled within the general education classroom setting and most often, will not result in expenses for the district or school. These accommodations can include; extending time for exams, shortening assignments in specific areas of study, provision of visual aids to assist with verbal instructions, and signing daily planners for assignment organization, or seating arrangement modifications. An exception to the financial restriction would be when an <u>access issue</u> presents itself. For example, if a disabled student requires a specific disability-related provision such as a hearing system for hearing impaired students, wheelchair entry or exit ramps for physically handicapped students, or special text books or materials for visually handicapped students; <u>cost should never be an issue</u>. All in all, a well written 504 Plan provides identified students with disabilities access to the same program typical General Education students are able to experience; however, accommodations are required as a result of the impairment.

*An extensive list of accommodations will be provided at the end of this section.

Unfortunately, due to the numbers game, such as class sizes bursting at the seams, epidemic like conditions creating special needs caseloads growing beyond expectations [i.e.; Autism, ADHD], and dwindling funding throughout the school system, IEP and 504 plans often require parents to push the envelope through advocacy, to assure the best services and accommodations possible for their children. First and foremost, advocacy is essential; for the focus on each individual student tends to get lost within the following process: An increasing number of students are identified with special needs, funding sources continue to decrease, and at the same time, an ever-expanding set of political pressures from local, state, and federal requirements are put upon schools to meet the needs of all students. As a result, school districts everywhere are backed into a corner to make due with so little resources so "one size fits all" instructional programs, cookie-cutter methodology, and rigid systems are created to manage this process overall. So you are thrown into a position you never imagined or asked for. As the education system plays out its own version of being caught between a rock and a hard place; you will be given the opportunity to be a beacon of light shining on your child's potential and promise within.

Connecting the Dots: Diagnosis + Present Levels = Support

As you move forward in this role as your child's advocate, you will be required to establish a solid case, evidence-based approach in support of his or her needs either through Section 504 or specially designed instruction via an IEP. Your starting point is grounded upon an air-tight hypothesis; connecting the dots between your child's poor academic achievement, and a defined disability based upon a diagnosis or suspected impairment, using either:

- A medical diagnosis and related evaluations completed through your own resources conducted outside of the school. Professionals such as Clinical Psychologists, Speech and Language Therapists, Occupational & Physical Therapists, and Counselors are just a few of the clinicians who may be able to support your hypothesis.
- A formal evaluation completed by the school district which may include a comparison between your child's ability through IQ-related tests, a battery of achievement tests, social-emotional-behavior surveys, and other assessments.

Most importantly, the process of qualifying for an IEP or 504 Plan may feel like an up-hill battle due to the one-size-fits-all nature of the intervention process. Certainly every school promotes the ideal of "doing what's best for students", however, as stress increases for those on the inside of the system, with a never-ending sense of responsibility for <u>every</u> student, often creativity, ingenuity, and innovation fall by the wayside. As a result, the following formula will guide you as you move forward; you should not take a detour from this advocacy path no matter what obstacles present themselves:

STEP ONE: (Diagnosis)

The diagnosis-disability needs to be mutually agreed upon and understood by staff members within the IEP and 504 Teams; your goal is to achieve **mutual understanding** across the table related to the foundation of your advocacy efforts; your hypothesis will always be in question if you cannot establish the fundamental reason for your child's lack of success in school. And this understanding may include social, emotional, behavior, physical, cognitive, and academic information to fully grasp mutual understanding. As a result, this may require you to invest in additional outside evaluations as your starting point.

For example:

- ADHD related symptoms can be highly inconvenient and disruptive to the classroom setting, and educators may not be informed of the processing related conditions which impair learning including: organization and planning gaps, cause and effect development hick-ups, impulsivity control, or working memory limitations. These insights are critical for many students on the ADD/ADHD spectrum for the distractibility issues and the inconvenience often takes precedent over the deeper cause of this condition and "behavior" takes over as the focus.
- AUTISM presents a wide-range of issues and behavioral impairments including social interaction and communication, expressive and receptive language, and hyper-focus issues. However, anxiety may be at the root of these behaviors and often gets lost in the discussion. It is imperative that anxiety is addressed as the team explores the behavioral implications of Autism. Again, the insights of a Clinical Psychologist may assist best in this area.
- Speaking of anxiety, ATTACHMENT is becoming an issue for so many students; not just a condition associated with Foster Care or Adoption. Social anxiety, emotional dysregulation, and relationships in general may present challenges for students experiencing attachment-related behaviors. The guidance from Counselors, Therapists, and Psychologists may best make the connection between the condition and learning so I recommend their insights. This is important when parents and teachers come together for relationship building strategies, and may need to be featured within intervention plans first and foremost in these situations.

STEP TWO: (Impact-Present Levels)

When describing the connection between the diagnosis/disability and its **impact on school and classroom performance**, you will need to strategically address the context of the evaluation(s) or diagnosis within the present levels of performance, as <u>observed</u> in the classroom or presented within data and academic assessments. It is necessary to illustrate these points through a wide angle lens; addressing academic, emotional, physical, and social considerations. Highlight your child's success, strengths, and talents demonstrated both in school and outside the school setting, in addition to the challenges demonstrated. And once again, if you cannot attain "mutual understanding" at this level through observations and an evidence-based approach, you will need to go back to the table with additional information including data from report cards, behavioral charts, assessments, formal tests, discipline documentation, and communication between home and school [i.e.; emails].

Then, once the IEP and 504 Teams are able to identify the connections between the disability and its impact as demonstrated within "present levels", the team will need to determine what are the goals, strategies, resources, and services to support your child:

STEP THREE: (Intervention-Support)

- **ACCOMMODATIONS (via 504 Plan or an IEP)**: General education accommodations and modifications which provide significant levels of support within the regular program. Based upon my experiences as a Principal and Advocate, 504 Plan accommodations may be difficult for parent advocates to negotiate. Though Section 504 Plan guidelines have been well established since 1973, as part of the Rehabilitation Act, there may be a vague understanding across the education landscape about 504 Plans and implementation tends to be interpreted within a spectrum of gray in contrast to an IEP. Specifically, there may be push back from staff and administrators for teachers often feel overwhelmed and the notion of individualizing within the classroom through accommodations for a specific student may create a defensive response from those who are asked to implement the plan. This is important to know. A compassionate, understanding, but also, an objective approach to advocacy makes a huge difference both in the development of a 504 Plan as well as following up on the implementation of the accommodations. Here again, an evidence-based approach to communication works best!

Within the context of a one-size-fits-all educational system, often basic accommodations are met with reluctance, including "I have 150-plus students, how can I accommodate for every student?" or "I have class size of 34 students, when am I going to have time to do this?" Nevertheless, the 504 and IDEA/IEP laws clearly support your child's need for modifications when a 504 plan or IEP is established. As a result, it's best to get in writing the most specific accommodations possible. Keep in mind, it would be valuable to know standard accommodations upfront before pursuing 504 accommodations as well as strategies for an IEP in advance of meeting with the team so you have a feel for what is reasonable and effective.

Guiding Questions: Accommodations

1. What is the specific accommodation?
2. How will it assist and support learning? Expected outcome?
3. How will the accommodation be implemented? (Be SPECIFIC)
4. When will it be implemented? Daily, Weekly, Monthly?
5. Who will be responsible for the accommodation and the follow through?
6. Where and under what conditions would one find the accommodation?
7. How will the success of accommodation be measure?

The following are basic accommodations associated with a wide-range of Learning Disabilities while additional links are provided for your review as well:

Presentation:

- Provide on audio tape Provide in large print

- Reduce number of items per page or line

- Provide a designated reader highlighting oral instruction or dictation.

Response:

- Allow for verbal responses

- Allow for answers to be dictated to a scribe

- Allow the use of a tape recorder to capture responses

- Permit responses to be given via computer

- Permit answers to be recorded directly into test booklet

Timing:

- Allow frequent breaks

- Extend allotted time for a test

- Extend allotted time for assignments and projects

Setting:

- Provide preferential seating

- Provide special lighting or acoustics

- Provide a space with minimal distractions

- Administer a test in small group setting or private room

Test Scheduling

- Administer a test in several timed sessions or over several days

- Allow subtests to be taken in a different order

- Administer a test at a specific time of day

- Provide special test preparation

- Provide on-task/focusing prompts

- **SPECIALLY DESIGNED INSTRUCTION (SDI) (via IEP):** When accommodations are not enough, SDI may be the means to support your child's success at school though one always moves through the "least restrictive" first. Allowing the general education accommodations opportunity to unfold before moving to specially designed instruction. However, an IEP may prove to be most effective within the intervention process for it is supported by compliance guidelines established at the state and district levels, and is founded upon an understanding associated with <u>clear-cut, black and white procedures and policies</u>. This is in direct contrast to Section 504 Plan policies and practices tends to be a bit fuzzy and possibly wishy-washy due to the general nature of the guidelines established at the federal level.

Elements of an IEP:

- Present Levels of Performance
- Goals establishing learning targets: Moving from Point A to Point B as Measured
- Accommodations provided within General Education setting and classes
- Service Matrix: Specially Designed Instruction and Minutes per service
- Transition Activities: For High School Students; "Long range plans after graduating"

Common Areas of Service:

- Reading
- Math
- Written Language
- Communication (Speech and Language)
- Occupational / Physical Therapy
- Social Skills
- Behavior

Summary: Guiding Questions

Information is everything. Know all you can about your child: Be the expert! Also, see your child through the same lens as the educators; working with the "Insider's Guide" will help make this presentation easier as you co-create mutual understanding across the table. Most notably, the IEP or 504 team needs to "get" the disability, and its impact on learning. The evaluation(s) and "present levels of performance" are the means to paint this picture of understanding. A well written evaluation from outside clinicians may prove to be your most valued tool, bar none! By connecting the dots between disability and your child's "present levels of performance"; the foundation of your advocacy hypothesis will unfold within your guidance.

Basically, the following questions will guide you as well as the overall process:

1. **Is there a disability or diagnosis identified by clinicians or licensed medical professionals?**

2. **How does this disability or diagnosis impact my son or daughter's school experience including academic, social, emotional, or behavior considerations?**

3. **Finally, how will Specially Designed Instruction through an IEP or General Education accommodations (Section 504 Plan) best support my child?**

Remember, as you make the decision to navigate through the school system, especially within the context of a special needs referral, you are playing on their home turf, so you need to tread carefully as a mindful guest, for all decisions do fall within their side of the court. Also, know that you have recourse when you do not agree with the decisions including: (See Procedural Safeguards)

- Independent Education Evaluation
- Mediation
- Due Process
- Citizens Complaint

And finally, due to the nature of education advocacy, with a focus on one child at a time, no two IEP or 504 Plans look alike due to the vast range of experiences, insights, and skill sets found at each school. Your point of reference is to establish the best plan possible given the conditions you are working with; there are no set in stone solutions to the process itself. As a result, you need to move forward till you can honestly say, "I have done my best ... and the team has done so as well".

Accommodation Guidelines:

State Guidelines follow Federal Law: The meaning of "disabled student" under Section 504 was substantially broadened by the Americans with Disabilities Amendments Act of 2008, which became effective on January 1, 2009. Congress amended the ADA in 2008 in the following specific ways to create "clear, strong, consistent, enforceable standards" to **broaden** who qualifies as a "disabled person" under Section 504 and the ADA.

Here is what the changes mean for schools:

1. Interpret the term "physical or mental impairment" broadly: The term "physical or mental impairment" is not limited to any specific diseases or categories of medical conditions;

2. Interpret the term "substantially limits" broadly: An impairment need not prevent, or significantly or severely restrict a student in performing a major life activity to be considered "substantially limiting." Compare a student to his or her non-disabled age/grade peers to determine whether an impairment substantially limits a major life activity for the student;

3. Interpret the term "major life activities" broadly: Just about any activity that is of importance to a school-aged student's daily life now qualifies as a "major life activity under Section 504 and an impairment that substantially limits one major life activity need not limit other major life activities in order to be considered a disability under Section 504 or the ADA;

4. Disregard mitigating measures used by a student: Mitigating measures used by a disabled student to manage his or her impairment or lessen the impact of his or her impairment (e.g. medication, medical devices, related aids and services, etc.) should be disregarded when determining whether a student's impairment constitutes a disability under Section 504 or the ADA;

5. Consider whether a temporary impairment is a disability: A temporary impairment (with an actual or expected duration of six months or less) is a disability under Section 504 and the ADA if it is severe enough that it substantially limits a major life activity for a student. The duration (or expected duration) of the impairment and the extent to which it actually limits a major life activity for a student should be the key considerations; and

6. Consider whether an impairment that is episodic or in remission is a disability: An impairment that is episodic or in remission (e.g. epilepsy, cancer, bipolar disorder, etc.) is a disability under Section 504 and the ADA if it substantially limits a major life activity for a student when active.

Sample Accommodations:

APPENDIX E ACCOMMODATION EXAMPLES FOR SPECIFIC DISABILITIES (*Puget Sound ESD*)

Here are some examples of accommodations and services that might be considered for specific disability profiles. Please keep in mind that these examples are not intended to be all inclusive or mandatory. Do not use these examples as a "checklist" as accommodations are to be made on a case-by-case basis specific to individual need. Please also remember that the mere presence of these conditions does not automatically qualify a student for a Section 504 plan. The disability must significantly limit one or more life functions before a Section 504 plan is to be considered. Additionally, this disability must impact the student so that he or she is not afforded access and benefit of programs and services equal to that of non-disabled students.

ALLERGIES EXAMPLE: The student has severe allergic reactions to certain pollens and foods. For purposes of this example the condition substantially limits the major life activity of breathing and may interfere with the student's ability to get to school or participate once there.

Possible Accommodations and Services: • Avoid allergy-causing substances: soap, weeds, pollen, food • In-service necessary persons: dietary people, peers, coaches, laundry service people, etc. • Allow time for shots/clinic appointments • Use air purifiers • Adapt physical education curriculum during high pollen time • Improve room ventilation (i.e., when remodeling has occurred and materials may cause an allergy) • Develop health care and/or emergency plans • Address pets/animals in the classroom • Involve school health consultant in school related health issues • Train for proper dispensing of medications; monitor and/or distribute medications; monitor for side effects

ARTHRITIS EXAMPLE: A student with severe arthritis may have persistent pain, tenderness or swelling in one or more joints. A student experiencing arthritic pain may require a modified physical education program. For purposes of this example, the condition substantially limits the major life activity of learning.

Possible Accommodations and Services: • Provide a rest period during the day • Accommodate for absences for doctors' appointments • Provide assistive devices for writing (e.g., pencil grips, non-skid surface, typewriter/computer, etc.) • Adapt physical education curriculum • Administer medication following medication administration protocols • Train student for proper dispensing of medications; monitor and/or distribute medications; monitor for side effects • Arrange for assistance with carrying books, lunch tray, etc. • Provide book caddie • Implement movement plan to avoid stiffness • Provide seating accommodations • Allow extra time between classes • Provide locker assistance • Provide modified eating utensils • Develop health care plan and emergency plan • Provide for accommodations for writing tasks: a note taker, a computer or tape recorder for note-taking • Make available access to wheelchair/ramps and school van for transportation • Provide more time for massage or exercises • Adjust recess time • Provide peer support groups • Arrange for instructional aide support • Install handle style door knobs (openers) • Record lectures/presentations • Have teachers provide outlines of presentations • Issue Velcro fasteners for bags • Obtain padded chairs • Provide a more comfortable style of desk • Adjust attendance policy, if needed • Provide a shorter school day • Furnish a warmer room and sit student close to the heat • Adapt curriculum for lab classes • Supply an extra set of books for home use and keep a set at school • Let student give reports orally rather than in writing • Provide an awareness program for staff and students • Monitor any special dietary considerations • Involve school health consultants in school health related issues • Provide post-secondary or vocational transition planning

ASTHMA EXAMPLE: A student has been diagnosed as having severe asthma. The doctor has advised the student not to participate in physical activity outdoors. For purposes of this example, the disability limits the major life activity of breathing.

Possible Accommodations and Services: • Adapt activity level for recess, physical education, etc. • Provide inhalant therapy assistance • Train for proper dispensing of medications; monitor and/or distribute medications; monitor for side • Remove allergens (e.g., hair spray, lotions, perfumes, paint, latex) • Make field trips that might aggravate the condition non-mandatory and supplement with videos, audiotapes, movies, etc. • Accommodate medical absence by providing makeup work, etc. • Adjust for administration of medications • Provide access to water, gum, etc. • Adapt curriculum expectations when needed (i.e., science class, physical education, etc.) • Develop health care and emergency plans • Have peers available to carry materials to and from classes (e.g., lunch tray, books) • Provide rest periods • Make health care needs known to appropriate staff • Provide indoor space for before and after school activities • Have a locker location which is centralized and free of atmosphere changes • Adapt attendance policies, school day duration, or 180-day requirement, if needed • Place student in most easily controlled environment

ATTENTION DEFICIT DISORDER (ADD) AND ATTENTION DEFICIT HYPERACTIVE DISORDER (ADHD) EXAMPLE: The student does not meet eligibility requirements under IDEA as emotionally disturbed, learning disabled, or other health impaired. A doctor regards the student as having ADD, and for purposes of this example, the disability limits the major life activity of learning. The student, because of his disability, is unable to participate in the school's programs to the same degree as students without disabilities and therefore is substantially limited by the disability.

Possible Accommodations and Services: • Seat the student away from distractions and in close proximity to the teacher • State classroom rules, post in an obvious location, and enforce consistently • Use simple, concise instructions with concrete steps • Provide seating options • Tolerate (understand the need) excessive movement • Provide a peer tutor/helper • Teach compensatory strategies • Train for proper dispensing of medications; monitor and/or distribute medications; monitor for side effects • Monitor for stress and fatigue; adjust activities • Adjust assignments to match attention span, etc. • Vary instructional pace • Vary instructional activities frequently • Provide supervision during transitions, disruptions, field trips • Model the use of study guides, organizing tools • Accommodate testing procedures; lengthy tests might be broken down into several shorter administrations • Provide counseling and prompt feedback on both successes and areas needing improvement • Initiate frequent parent communication • Establish a school/home behavior management program • Provide training for staff • Have the student use an organizer; train in organizational skills • Establish a nonverbal cue between teacher and student for behavior monitoring • Assign chores/duties around room/school • Adapt environment to avoid distractions • Reinforce appropriate behavior • Have child work alone or in a study carrel during high stress times • Highlight required or important information/directions • Provide a checklist for student, parents, and/or teacher to record assignments of completed tasks • Use a timer to assist student to focus on given task or number of problems in time allotted; stress that problems need to be done correctly. • Have student restate or write directions/instructions • Allow student to respond in variety of different modes (i.e., may place answers for tests on tape instead of paper) • Give student opportunity to stand/move while working • Provide additional supervision to and from school • Adapt student's work area to help screen out distracting stimuli • Grade for content integrity not just neatness/presentation • Schedule subjects which require greater concentration early in the day • Supply small rewards to promote behavior change • Avoid withholding physical activity as a negative reinforcer • Allow for periodic, frequent physical activity, exercise, etc. • Determine trigger points and prevent action leading to trigger points • Provide for socialization opportunities, such as circle of friends

BIPOLAR DISORDER EXAMPLE: The student was diagnosed as having a bipolar disorder, however the severity (frequency, intensity, duration considerations) of the condition did not qualify the student for IDEA. A properly convened Section 504 committee determined that the condition did significantly impair the major life activity of learning and fashioned a Section 504 plan for the student.

Possible Accommodations and Services: • Break down assignments into manageable parts with clear and simple directions, given one at a time • Plan advanced preparation for transitions • Monitor clarity of understanding and alertness • Allow most difficult subjects at times when student is most alert • Provide extra time on tests, class work, and homework if needed • Strategies in place for unpredictable mood swings • Provide appropriate staff with training on bipolar disorder. • Create awareness by staff of potential victimization from other student • Implement a crisis intervention plan for extreme cases where student gets out of control and may do something impulsive or dangerous • Provide positive praise and redirection • Report any suicidal comments to counselor/psychologist immediately • Consider home instruction for times when the student's mood disorder makes it impossible for him to attend school for an extended period

CANCER EXAMPLE: A student with a long-term medical problem may require special accommodations. Such a condition as cancer may substantially limit the major life activities of learning and caring for oneself. For example, a student with cancer may need a class schedule that allows for rest and recuperation following chemotherapy.

Possible Accommodations and Services: • Adjust attendance policies • Limit numbers of classes taken; accommodate scheduling needs (breaks, etc.) • Send teacher/tutor to hospital, as appropriate • Take whatever steps are necessary to accommodate student's involvement in extracurricular activities if they are otherwise qualified • Adjust activity level and expectations in classes based on physical limitations; don't require activities that are too physically taxing • Train for proper dispensing of medications; monitor and/or distribute medications; monitor for side effects • Provide appropriate assistive technology • Provide dietary accommodations • Provide a private area in which to rest • Shorten school day • Arrange for home tutoring following treatment • Send additional set of texts and assignments to hospital schools • Tape lessons. Accept the fact that the lessons and content-area tests may not be appropriate; the student is learning many life lessons through this experience • Adjust schedule to include rest breaks • Provide counseling; establish peer group support • Adapt physical education • Provide access to school health services • Provide awareness training to appropriate staff and students • Develop health care emergency plan to deal with getting sick at school • Offer counseling for death and dying to peers/teachers/staff • Furnish a peer tutor • Provide student with a student buddy for participation in sports • Initiate a free pass system from the classroom • Provide lessons using mastery learning techniques • Provide individual school counseling • Begin friendship groups for the student • Provide teachers with counseling, emphasizing positive attitudes • Have a health plan for care of mediport/any other intravenous lines and medical needs • Plan ongoing communication about school events • Notify parents of communicable diseases in school • Designate a person in school to function as liaison with parents as a means of updating changing health status

CEREBRAL PALSY EXAMPLE: The student has serious difficulties with fine and gross motor skills. A wheelchair is used for mobility. For purposes of this example, the condition substantially limits the major life activity of walking. Cognitive skills are intact.

Possible Accommodations and Services: • Provide assistive technology devices • Arrange for use of ramps and elevators • Allow for extra time between classes • Assist with carrying books, lunch trays, etc. • Adapt physical education curriculum • Provide for physical therapy as appropriate. Such therapy needs to relate directly to "life skills" • Train for proper dispensing of medications; monitor and/or distributed medications; monitor for side effects • Adapt eating utensils • Initiate a health care plan that also addresses emergency situations • Train paraprofessionals in the case of this student (i.e. feeding, diapering, transporting to and from the wheelchair) • Adapt assignments • Educate peers/staff with parent/student permission • Ensure that programs conducted in the basement or on second or third floor levels are accessible • Ensure that bathroom facilities, sinks and water fountains are readily accessible. • Provide post-secondary or vocational transition planning.

CHRONIC INFECTIOUS DISEASES i.e., Acquired Immune Deficiency Syndrome (AIDS) EXAMPLE: The student frequently misses school and does not have the strength to attend a full day. For purposes of this example, the student has a record of a disability, which substantially limits the major life activities of learning. Please review applicable District policies.

Possible Accommodations and Services: • In-service staff and students about the disease, how it is transmitted and how it is treated (Consult appropriate District policies) • Apply universal precautions • Administer medications following medication administration protocols, train for proper dispensing of medications; monitor and/or distribute medications; monitor for side effects • Adjust attendance policies • Adjust schedule or shorten day • Provide rest periods • Adapt physical education curriculum • Establish routine communication with health professionals, area nurse, and home • Develop health-care and emergency plan • Consult with doctor, parents, teachers, area nurse, and administrators • Train appropriate teachers on medical/emergency procedures • Provide two-way audio/video link between home and classroom via computer, etc. • Arrange for an adult tutor at school or home • Adapt assignments and tests • Provide an extra set of textbooks for home • Provide staff training on confidentiality • Provide education and support for peers regarding issues of death and dying • Provide transportation to and from school if needed as a related service • Tape books or provide a personal reader • Arrange to communicate with a home computer with e-mail • Notify parents of communicable disease in the classroom • Arrange for participation in a support group • Provide for post-secondary employment transitions for secondary students • Foster supportive community attitudes regarding the District's need to provide education to HIV positive/AIDS students • Develop and promote a nondiscriminatory classroom climate and supportive student attitudes • Promote the most supportive, least restrictive educational program • Initiate a "Kids on the Block" AIDS program • Videotape classroom teaching • Provide a peer support group to encourage communication • Involve school health consultant in school-related health issues

CYSTIC FIBROSIS EXAMPLE: This student is a new enrollee at your school and has an extensive medical history. He has significant difficulty breathing and will often be absent due to respiratory infection. While medical needs can be easily documented on a health plan, his educational needs also need to be accommodated. For purposes of this example, learning is the major life activity that is substantially impaired.

Possible Accommodations and Services: • Train for proper dispensing of medications; monitor and/or distribute medications; monitor for side effects • Create a health care plan for management of acute and chronic phases • Promote good communication between parents, hospital, home, and school on school assignments • Shorten the school day • Adapt physical education activities • Apply universal precautions, correct disposal of fluids • Recognize need for privacy for "good coughing" • Educate staff and peers

DEAF/HEARING IMPAIRMENT EXAMPLE: A student was diagnosed with a substantial hearing impairment at a very early age. Therefore, he has both a hearing loss and a mild speech impediment. He compensates through both lip reading and sign language. Academic abilities test in the average range.

Possible Accommodations and Services: • Allow for written direction/instructions in addition to oral presentation • Ensure delivery of instruction facing the student to allow lip reading • Provide visual information as primary mode of instruction • Allow for provision of interpreter services • Install acoustical tile, carpeting • Seat in a location with minimal background noise • Provide paper and pencil/pen to write/draw requests when needed • Facilitate acquisition of TDDs and related assistive technology • Allow for extra time between classes • Provide post-secondary or vocational transition planning

DIABETES EXAMPLE: A sixth grader with juvenile diabetes requires accommodation to maintain optimal blood sugar. His mom provides the crackers and juice to be used at "break" time and before physical education class. She asks that teachers remind him to eat at a certain time of the morning if he does not pay attention to the beeper on his watch. The youngster is very self-sufficient; while he is able to monitor his own blood sugar now, he prefers to do this privately. Therefore, mom asks that the equipment and a notebook/log be stored in a nearby file cabinet and the youngster be allowed to go into the hall with the equipment to check his blood sugar twice a day. She also asks that his teacher allow him to use the bathroom as needed.

Possible Accommodations and Services: • Health care plan for management of condition in the school setting and in emergencies • Educate staff to signs/symptoms of insulin reaction/hypoglycemia; hunger, shakiness, sweatiness, change in face color, disorientation, drowsiness • Do not leave the child alone if he/she is feeling poorly; walk to the office or clinic with the student. • Train for proper dispensing of medications; monitor and/or distribute medications; monitor for side effects; communicate systematically and frequently with parents • Adapt physical education activities • Store equipment and documentation in a readily accessible location for student, parent, and area nurse or clinic aid • Accommodate food access/meal schedules rigorously • Allow access to bathroom facilities

DRUGS AND ALCOHOL EXAMPLE: The student has used drugs and alcohol for many years. This problem has affected the major life activities of learning and caring for oneself. The student is presently not using drugs or alcohol and is in a rehabilitation program. If the student is not using drugs or alcohol, he or she could qualify for accommodations or services under Section 504.

Possible Accommodations and Services: • Provide copies of texts and assignments to treatment facility • Arrange for periodic home-school contacts • Establish daily/weekly assignments monitoring system • Communicate with treatment facility; pursue transition services available through the treatment facility • Provide/arrange for counseling • Establish peer support group • Dismiss from school for treatment without punitive measures • Ensure strong link with school counselor • Arrange for access to treatment at private or public facilities. • Integrate a student assistance program into the classroom • In-service faculty/staff with parent/student permission •

Provide post-secondary or vocational transition planning • Provide ongoing support around chemical dependency in conjunction with other agencies • Train for proper dispensing of medications; monitor and/or distribute medications; monitor for side effects

EMOTIONALLY DISTURBED EXAMPLE: An emotionally disturbed student may need an adjusted class schedule to allow time for regular counseling or therapy. For purposes of this example, the condition substantially limits the individual's major life activity of learning.

Possible Accommodations and Services: • Train for proper dispensing of medications; monitor and/or distribute medications; monitor for side effects • Maintain weekly/daily journals for self-recording of behavior • Establish home-school communication system • Schedule periodic meetings with home and treatment specialists • Provide carry-over of treatment plans into school environment • Assist with inter-agency referrals • Utilize behavior management programs • Develop contracts for student behavior • Post rules for classroom behaviors; teach expectations • Provide counseling, social skills instruction • Reinforce replacement behaviors • Educate other students/staff/school personnel • Foster carryover of treatment plans to home environment • Reinforce positive behavior • Schedule shorter study/work periods according to attention span capabilities • Be consistent in setting expectations and following up on reinforcements/consequences • Provide post-secondary or vocational transition planning

ENCOPRESIS/ENURESIS EXAMPLE: A student who will urinate or defecate in clothes. Not to be confused with physical incontinence, but only to a needed behavior change (i.e. toilet training, bowel/bladder retraining).

Possible Accommodations: • Maintain low key responses • Have a change of clothes available at school in the clinic or alternative location • Plan a consistent response to events; send student to clinic or alternative location for cleanup and change of clothes; while wearing latex/rubber gloves, place soiled clothes in a plastic bag; call parent and make arrangements for soiled items to be returned home • Observe for consistent trigger events • Support bowel/bladder retraining program that is recommended by the physician

EPILEPSY EXAMPLE: The student is on medication for seizure activity, but experiences several petit mal seizures each month. This condition substantially limits the major life activity of learning.

Possible Accommodations and Services: • Call parent and document the characteristics of each seizure • Assess breathing after seizure • Train for proper dispensing of medications; monitor and/or distribute medications; monitor for side effects • Train staff and students and prepare an emergency plan • Anticipate recovery process should a seizure occur. Move seating/clear space during seizure. Do not insert objects into the student's mouth during seizure; administer no fluids if student is unconscious. Turn the unconscious student on his or her side to avoid aspiration of vomit. Provide rest time and return to academic considerations following seizure. • Arrange a buddy system, especially for field trips • Avoid portable chalk boards or furniture that would topple over easily • Provide an alternative recess, adapt activities such as climbing and/or swimming • Plan for academic make-up work • Alter door openings to allow access from the outside (i.e., bathroom stall doors that swing both ways) • Observe for consistent triggers (e.g., smells, bright light, perfume, hair spray) • Provide post-secondary or vocational transition planning

HEARING IMPAIRMENT EXAMPLE: A parent is hearing impaired and requests, access to school sponsored activities. The District makes accommodations by providing interpreter services for the parent to participate effectively in school-sponsored events or meetings about the student.

Possible Accommodations and Services: • Provide an interpreter for those school events where accommodations may be necessary/are requested • Make alternative arrangements for home-school contacts/communication • Assist with locating peer or support groups • Use written notes for communication • Arrange with phone company for assistive devices on public phones • Provide information on assistive technology; acquire assistive equipment for school use • Provide in-house TDD or relay services to receive/communicate efficiently • Provide post-secondary or vocational transition planning

LEARNING DISABILITIES EXAMPLE: (*Individual profiles of learning strengths and weaknesses will vary*). The student has a learning disability that impacts her ability to read. She has more difficulty with word decoding and spelling than reading comprehension. Thus, completing reading tasks is difficult and slow. She is currently a student receiving special education services.

Possible Accommodations and Services: • Provide lower-readability materials covering course context • Provide extended time on tests • Arrange for student/volunteer readers • Provide information on accessing materials through recordings for the Blind and Dyslexic (i.e., books on tape) • Allow access to spell checkers and/or word processing • Provide information on accommodations for college-entrance/qualifying exams (i.e., PSAT) • Written directions in addition to oral • Clearly sequenced instruction • Visual graphs/charts/diagrams to support instruction • Provision of computer access • Seating toward the instructor • Support/suggestions relative to post-secondary/career options • Support in the use of organizational/time-management • Support in the use of strategies to assist memory and problem-solving • Use of multi-sensory instructional methods (i.e., visual graphs and charts to accompany oral presentation) • Provide post-secondary or vocational transition planning

LEUKEMIA EXAMPLE: The student has recently been diagnosed with leukemia and requires frequent hospitalization. The condition substantially limits the major life activity of learning and caring for oneself.

Possible Accommodations and Services: • Involve area nurse in assessing current limitations and development of health plan • Provide homebound instruction if needed • Provide the student with an adjusted school day • Make needed accommodations during physical education/recess • Provide rest periods • Have medical services and medication available at school. Train for proper dispensing of medications; monitor and/or distribute medications; monitor for side effects • Support the proper diet as per physical recommendation • With parent/student permission, have area nurse to educate teachers/staff/peers • Notify parents of existing communicable diseases at school (i.e., chicken pox, flu, strep throat, etc.) • Consult with medical staff about individual needs and/or concomitant factors

ORTHOPEDICALLY IMPAIRED EXAMPLE: The student has limited mobility and uses a wheelchair. This condition substantially limits the major life activity of walking.

Possible Accommodations and Services: • Develop a health care and emergency plan • Implement an adaptive physical education program • Provide physical therapy at school • Correct problems with physical accessibility of facilities/pathways between buildings • Provide extra time to get to class • Supply a set of textbooks for home • Provide a copy of class notes from a peer • Practice emergency exit from school building • Ensure that access to programs held in the basement or on second or third floors is handicapped accessible • Ensure that bathroom facilities, water fountains, sinks, etc. are readily accessible • Provide post-secondary or vocational transition planning

STUDENT WITH SPECIAL HEALTH CARE NEEDS EXAMPLE: The student has a special health care problem and requires clean intermittent catheterization twice each day. This procedure empties the bladder and helps prevent urinary tract infections and possible wetting. The school is required to provide trained personnel to perform the procedure or to provide the student a private location to perform the procedure. The condition is substantially limiting in the major life activity of caring for oneself.

Possible Accommodations and Services: • Apply universal precautions • Provide trained personnel to perform special medical procedures. Train for proper dispensing of medications; monitor and/or distribute medications; monitor for side effects • Provide student with private location and time to perform procedures • Involve area nurse, parents, teachers, and staff in periodic review • Allow preferential seating as indicated by need • Adapt recess, physical education, and transportation • Adjust classroom environment • Develop health care and emergency plan • If necessary, adapt attendance policy • Establish health alert system whereby every staff member involved with this student is aware of the health problem and of proper procedures • Provide a beeper/paging system for trained personnel • Make available homebound services/instruction if needed • Provide school counseling • Arrange for in-service to other students and staff with parent/student permission • Provide post-secondary or vocational transition planning

TEMPORARILY DISABLED EXAMPLE: A student was in an automobile accident and will be homebound and/or hospitalized for an extensive period. The student is considered temporarily disabled under Section 504 and should receive accommodations if this disability substantially limits a major life activity for the period of time it does so.

Possible Accommodations and Services: • Provide duplicate sets of texts • Provide assignments to hospital school • Tape lessons • Provide homebound instruction • Schedule periodic home-school meetings • Arrange for student to leave class early to get to next class • Provide access to elevators • Excuse from or adapt physical education program • Arrange for a friend to assist student in getting from class to class, provide help with getting lunch tray • Establish a student support network • Provide a cordless telephone/beeper/pager • Provide an interactive system -- computer, e-mail, TV • Arrange for peer notes • Change seating arrangements to accommodate needs • Adapt assignments depending on disability • Allow more time for test completion • Allow shortened days; adjust attendance policy • In-service staff and class and prepare an emergency care plan • Switch programs/classes to an accessible classroom on the main floor • Test verbally • Provide peer assistance for social involvement (i.e., to keep child informed of social activities) • Furnish life-skill assistance • Provide area nurse services

TOURETTE'S SYNDROME EXAMPLE: The student exhibits inappropriate gestures and sounds in the classroom and hallways. The condition is substantially limiting in the major life activities of learning and caring for oneself.

Possible Accommodations and Services: • Provide student with a means of catching up on missed lessons • Pair with a fellow student for study if indicated • Educate other students about associated outbursts/gestures/tics • Arrange for frequent parental interaction if indicated • Monitor administration/side effects of medication • Implement a behavior management program if indicated; cue student about inappropriate behaviors • Provide supervision for transition activities, during periods of "acting out" • Provide alternative/larger work space or appropriate space for the child to act out if indicated • Teach compensatory strategies • Adapt assignments if indicated • Provide peer/teacher in-service with parent/student permission • Provide post-secondary or vocational transition planning

TRAUMATIC BRAIN INJURY EXAMPLE: The student sustained a brain injury in an automobile accident. Many academic and motor skills have been lost from the injury. The student does not qualify for special education under IDEA. The condition is substantially limiting to the major life activities of learning and performing manual tasks.

Possible Accommodations and Services: • Provide extended school year/time • Furnish memory/organizational aids • Provide alternative testing • Initiate tutoring programs • Arrange an emergency plan • Monitor for seizure activity • In-service staff and peers with student/parent permission • Monitor fatigue/mental exhaustion • Provide frequent short breaks during periods of intense concentration • Shorten the instructional day if indicated • Provide strategies for organizing/sequencing tasks • Provide post-secondary or vocational transition planning

TUBERCULOSIS EXAMPLE: The student is suspected of having active tuberculosis and must stay home until diagnostic tests are completed. The disease is no longer infectious, but the student is still weak. The condition is substantially limiting to the major life activity of learning.

Possible Accommodations and Services: • Provide home tutor, as necessary • In-service staff on the need for confidentiality to limit the stigmatization of him or her • Have the medical evaluator provide feedback to staff • Train for proper dispensing of medications; monitor and/or distribute medications; monitor for side effects • In-service staff and students about the disease, how it is transmitted, and how it is treated • Work with community agency or health department to provide medication and health education materials • Work with community agency or health department to test students and staff for exposure and/or infection and to determine when the student can return to school • Provide therapy and dispense medications if student is diagnosed with active TB; observed for side effects; arrange for parents to give medication on holidays and weekends

VISUAL IMPAIRMENT EXAMPLE: A student has a progressive medical disorder, which results in increasing loss of visual acuity. He now requires both enhanced lighting and enlarged print materials in order to read.

Possible Accommodations and Services: • Preferential seating • Adaptations to the physical environment (i.e., consistent room arrangement, removal of obstacles to path of entry) • Copies of text/reading materials for adaptation • Modified writing tools (i.e., dark felt tip pens) • Perkins Brailler • Slate and stylus • Raised lines on writing paper • Dark lined writing paper • Lighting aids • Low vision devices including magnifiers, monocular glass, closed-circuit TV • Desktop Slant Board • Enlarged print materials; textbooks, workbooks, worksheets • Braille textbooks/reading materials • Books on tape • Audiotape recorder, tapes and organizational location (headphones if needed) • Oral instead of written tests • Standardized tests (i.e., CAT, SAT) in large print or Braille •

Tactile maps • Computer with enlarged print screen/adaptations • Speech synthesizer for input and output • Screen reading device • Optical Character Recognition System Scanner • Mobility devices (i.e., white cane) • Abacus

WEIGHT: DIAGNOSIS OF OBESITY, ANOREXIA, And BULIMIA EXAMPLE: A student has an extreme eating disorder that may require special accommodations. Obesity may be considered a disability under Section 504 where it substantially impairs a major life activity or is regarded by others as doing so.

Possible Accommodations and Services: • Provide special seating modifications • Make dietary modifications per physician recommendation • Adapt physical education program per physician recommendation • Allow extra time to get to classes • Educate peers • Adapt rest rooms • Provide opportunities for socialization and peer counseling/interaction • Ensure privacy for self-care • Provide counseling involving the area nurse • Provide for elevator privileges per physician's recommendation • Arrange for counselor/area nurse to supervise peer counseling to deal with esteem issues, peer attitudes, teasing, etc. • Address busing concerns to ensure room on buses for seating • Arrange to provide opportunities for the individual to participate in intramural and extracurricular events • Make any class location changes that may be needed.

A Parent & Educator Guide to Free Appropriate Public Education - 62 - Puget Sound ESD, Office of Special Services, March, 2010

Before the Meeting:

Doing the Homework

The majority of the cases I work with are founded upon previously diagnosed medical conditions or disabilities impacting the school experience and specifically, learning (see below). I find it much easier to establish a connection between a medical diagnosis [i.e.; ADHD, Autism, Down Syndrome], or an established Learning Disability [i.e.; Reading, Writing, Math, Communication, Speech], rather than working from scratch. Coming into the conversation with a professionally developed diagnosis from an outside clinician assists in creating consensus or a mutual understanding rather than working from a general – non-specific position: "My son is not doing well in school" or "He just doesn't get good grades" versus "My daughter has an ADHD diagnosis" or "My daughter has been diagnosed with Autism since Pre-School". Jumping into the IEP and 504 Plan arenas with a non-specific cause of poor academic achievement may encourage the school to respond with a broad stroke hypothesis of their own such as "lack of motivation", "laziness", "poor attendance", "developmentally will catch up", or an implied "lack of parental guidance". Nevertheless, one can enter the process without a hypothesis but you will need to establish a compelling reason for the school to begin testing and evaluate for a disability by connecting the dots through an evidence-based approach leading toward understanding: report cards, classroom test scores, district assessments, disciplinary notices, and emails between home and school.

Develop Your Hypothesis

As stated, it is much easier to move forward when a diagnosis has already been established by a professional from the medical/mental health community. For example, when I am working with foster care cases, I work from the hypothesis that many foster children experience a number of learning challenges including: attachment issues (RAD), ADD/ADHD attention issues, and anxiety disorders and research clearly supports this premise. When addressing ADD/ADHD, "working memory" or "processing" related Executive Functioning issues are at the core of the developmental issues in the school setting. Within Autism Spectrum cases, "sensory processing", "social skill development", and "hyper-focus" issues are classic conditions to build a hypothesis upon.

Remember, your primary purpose is to lead the discussion from perception to evaluation, subjective to objective, by letting the facts speak for themselves. Do your homework before meeting with the team. Establish a basis why your child struggles at school through a hypothesis as follows:

If you have a pre-determined diagnosis or disability:

"My child's success at school appears to be significantly impacted by…"

- ADD/ADHD
- Autism / Asperger syndrome
- Depression / Anxiety
- Oppositional Defiance
- Separation Anxiety
- Sleep disorder
- Specific Learning Disability: Reading, Writing, Math, Communication (Speech/Language)

Demonstrate the impact of disability through a review of the evidence (see Making Your Case)

If you do not have a pre-determined disability or diagnosis, the following conversation may need to be developed based upon the impact supported by a backlog of evidence:

"My child struggles in school and I would like to pursue an evaluation to determine the cause of his or her lack of success":

The following set of evidence will guide you as you make your case:

- Report cards
- Classroom test scores
- District assessments
- Disciplinary notices,
- Emails between home and school
- Other documents: _____

Make Your Case: The Cum File

Review your child's formal records by asking the Office Manager or School Secretary for the "cumulative file" [i.e.; Cum File, sounds like "fume" with a C]. This is the official record of your child's academic progress available for your review. If your child is new to your school, it may take 6-8 weeks for this to be sent from the former school so you may need to ask a staff member in the office to follow up with the former school and request a rush on the file.

This is a treasure chest of documentation supporting your hypothesis and you will likely find:

- Report Cards from Kindergarten through Grade 12
- Previous Title I or "LAP" Plans*, 504 Plans, or IEP related documents
- Discipline notes, suspensions, and referrals (ask for copies)
- State Assessments: i.e.; ITBS (3rd, 6th, 8th), STAR, MSP, SBAC
- Reading, math, writing assessments (district mandated)
- Other important information: _____

Take notes and make copies in support of your findings. Keep in mind: It may take the office staff a few days to copy the documents you are finding within the file; best to not push this request too hard for you don't want to make this an inconvenience for anyone if you can.

Identify all support materials which provide evidence aligned with your hypothesis. Connect the dots between disability and performance for example:

Report Cards: "Joanie fails to turn in work" (teachers' comments)

Tests: "Fails to meet standards in math" (State and District assessments)

Emails: Anything and everything written by teachers or staff: "He is off-task"

Discipline records: Suspensions, class room time-outs

Work Samples: Show real class assignments establishing impact if available in the "Cum Folder'"; you will likely need to access classroom based evidence through your child's teacher. (See below)

Meet Your Child's Teacher(s):

Meet or call your child's teacher(s) and check in with them to assure you know exactly where they stand on your "hypothesis"; establish allies. You are trying to identify "insiders" who also see your child's struggles as you do.

With a disability or diagnosis on record (whether with an IEP or for the 1st time):

"I believe my son/daughter continues to struggle in school because of ____ disability. How do you see it in the classroom?"

Without a disability or diagnosis on record:

"I believe my son/daughter struggles in school. How do you see it in the classroom?"

- Ask for specific work samples or incidents for future reference.
- Ask them what they are comfortable with presenting at the future meetings.
- Send them an email to thank them for their support and restate as follows:
  - *"Thank you for your time yesterday. The highlights from our conversation include"*:
  - Restate their insights about your child and the challenges she/he faces; be specific.

Keep all emails and records of all phone calls for future use; these emails will prove to be most valuable when you are presenting evidence for the present levels in the 504 or IEP meetings. Trust me on this! Staff members may have a propensity to change their story from informal conversations to formal meeting discussions. And you want the paper trail of emails to support your advocacy position.

Also, contact all other staff members who have an established relationship with your child and follow the procedures above. Consider the following as you establish your team of allies:

- Specialists: PE, Music, Art, Speech and Language, Gifted Education
- Principal: Primarily seeking all copies of disciplinary action including suspensions, formal "time outs", and school-wide referrals.
- Counselor
- Other:_____ _____ _____ _____

Know Your Target: Qualifying for Support

As stated earlier, there are two primary intervention options available for students with disabilities:

ACCOMMODATIONS (via 504 Plan or an IEP): General education accommodations and modifications provide significant levels of support within the regular program; Accommodations alone are supported through a 504 Plan. Based upon my experiences as a Principal and Advocate, 504 Plan accommodations may be most difficult for parent advocates to negotiate. Though Section 504 Plan guidelines have been well established since 1973, as part of the Rehabilitation Act, there may be a vague understanding across the education landscape about 504 Plans and implementation tends to be interpreted within a spectrum of gray in contrast to an IEP.

SPECIAL EDUCATION/IEP: Specially-Designed Instruction (SDI*) through services beyond the regular classroom accommodations. Example: Study Skills Center, Math Lab, Small Reading Groups, Instructional Assistant support. Qualification categories include Specific Learning Disabilities* [reading, math, writing, communication]. Health Impairment, and other specific qualification categories like autism, blind, hearing, intellectual, orthopedic, traumatic brain injury do not need a "discrepancy" to qualify, however, each needs to be supported by a significant impact when one compares a disabled student's performance compared to a neuro-typical student at the same grade level.

*Specific Learning Disability (SLD) Most often demonstrating a discrepancy (difference) between ability and achievement:

- Reading
- Written Language
- Math
- Communication: Speech and Language
- Occupational and Physical Therapy

Example: The ability and achievement tests determining Special Education eligibility within a SLD category would typically need to show a minimum of a 15 -20 point difference in scores when qualifying for specially designed instruction (IEP). Both WISC (IQ: "ability") vs. WIAT /WJR tests ("achievement") are standard assessment utilized to qualify but the Evaluation process determining eligibility is not limited to these tests alone.

Specific Learning Disabilities: Sample Discrepancy Model:

WISC - IQ: (average score 90-110)   Example: Full Scale score = 105

WIAT - Achievement: (using the same scale: average range 90-110)

- Reading: a score of 91 would NOT be a qualifying score; only 14 point discrepancy.
- Written Language: a score of 83 MAY be a qualifying score; a 22 point
- Math: a score of 95 would NOT be a qualifying score; only a 10 point discrepancy.

Also, student may receive specially designed instruction via an IEP if the team utilizes professional judgment to trump the discrepancy issue. This is important to know for the full scale IQ score on a WISC often does not reflect the true story of a child's disability especially in cases where processing speed or working memory are issues. This will be addressed later in the handbook.

Health Impairment:

Health Impairment includes: asthma, ADD/ADHD, diabetes, epilepsy, a heart condition, hemophilia, lead poisoning, leukemia, nephritis, rheumatic fever, sickle cell anemia, and other conditions adversely affecting a child's educational performance. The qualification guidelines with Health Impairment do not require a discrepancy between ability and achievement scores. Nevertheless, your "evidence-based" data collection will be most valuable in addressing instructional needs. So I would recommend both cognitive and academic achievement assessments within a formal Evaluation to truly capture understanding how processing is impacted through ADD/ADHD.

Specifically, when addressing ADD/ADHD, the following information within your data collection may prove to be most critical in consideration:

- WISC: <u>Working Memory</u> [the ability to process information, especially the amount of short-term information and one's ability to access the information when performing tasks requiring access to this stored memory].
- WIAT/WJR: Processing Related subtests: <u>Reading Comprehension</u>, <u>Math Problem Solving</u>, and <u>Written Expression.</u>

  These areas within the assessment often require handling multiple steps as well as a wide range of stored memory; *working memory* often causes gaps in these areas:

  - *Reading*: Many kids can make the sound-symbol recognition but the ability to apply this information within the context of a story may prove to be too complex; transferring memory from one task to another, and holding on to each element can be a challenge.

  - *Math*: Also, students with ADD/ADHD often struggle with the multiple steps required of math problem solving and overall understanding of math concepts if asked to write about their understanding of the process. Again, students who experience Working Memory challenges often struggle with transferring memory from one process, like calculation, and applying it within the larger picture of a math word problem, which requires multiple tasks including reading comprehension.

  - *Written Language*: This can also be an area of great struggle for students experiencing who find it difficult to initiate idea development, cannot put their thoughts around a topic of little or no meaning, or develop a block when their ideas move to the paper.

This also can be compounded by another element of ADD/ADHD referred to as "organization and planning" (see Executive Functioning). For many students on the ADD/ADHD spectrum, the ability to develop well thought cause and relationship connections, organize information within easily retrievable categories, or remain focused amidst distractions are challenging. It is not about distractibility alone as if it's a matter of making bad choices. There's a number of brain-related processes going on!

Autism and Other Specific Disabilities:

Unlike Specific Learning Disabilities, students with an Autism and other disabilities often do not have cognitive and achievement assessments within their profile for the identifying process does not require a discrepancy based decision between the two tests. However, an evaluation highlighted by both IQ and achievement test data would certainly help the team better understand the student's strengths as well as challenges. If possible, and appropriate, the following assessments may pose valuable information:

- WISC: <u>Processing Speed:</u> [Processing speed has to do with how quickly a person is able to carry out simple or automatic cognitive tasks; usually this is measured under time pressure such that a degree of focused attention is involved]. Many students on the Autism Spectrum are impacted due to their innate ability to deeply process concepts; as a result, many students on the spectrum need additional time to process their thought-processes. While typical students are able to multi-task and move superficially from one concept to another, if one is on the spectrum, moving at a rabbit's pace may be a challenge when your brain naturally moves at a turtle's pace.

- WIAT/WJR: Due to the hyper-focus attributes found with the spectrum, the WIAT/WJR achievement tests may highlight important instructional targets to build curriculum around. For example, many students with an Autism diagnosis benefit from an "interest-based" connection to learning. So if you are able to design accommodations based upon one's strengths, this type of intervention may go far. On the other side of the coin, many students on the spectrum struggle with writing. Assessments like the WJR or WIAT may help create better understanding to build upon what actually works and the instructional intervention team can move from this point forward. I personally have attended hundreds of IEP meetings where students developed such as high level of anxiety related to writing just the sight of a pen causes one to shut down and a diagnosis of dysgraphia plays out.

Establish Present Levels of Performance: The Homework

Within IEP (Special Education) and 504 Plan (General Education) support models, your ability to advocate for accommodations or additional resources for your child will be founded upon what is called "Present Levels of Performance"; by establishing a clear understanding of the following considerations based upon your child's current conditions: *Academic, Cognitive, Emotional, Physical, Social, and Behavioral:*

1. Your child's strengths
2. Connecting the dots between the disability-diagnosis and its impact on the considerations

You may be provided the opportunity to present your son or daughter's profile to a team of school personnel and help them see your child from a holistic perspective*; you are painting an accurate and compelling portrait of your child's achievement highlighting intellectual/academic, social, emotional, and physical-based evidence. Also, if your child is already receiving support via a 504 Plan or IEP, it would be most helpful to identify the current goals, services, and expected outcomes related to each area of support within the "present levels".

Many parents feel there is a tendency for staff to minimize the conditions impacting learning and generalize the causes. As a result, it is imperative that you enter the negotiation process with extensive information about your child and function as "the expert". The following suggestions will make a significant difference as you advocate on your child's behalf. Let me say this again, "Present Levels of Performance" (the "what" and the "why") function as the foundation for your advocacy! Be compelling and prepared to exhibit evidence; a direct connection between the disability/diagnosis and the impact on learning through the present levels, by doing the homework/research!

* *The initial request for an Evaluation, leading to a 504 Plan or IEP, may be addressed within a staff-only meeting. If so, make sure your hypothesis and supporting documentation are well-written; share with a representing staff member prior to the meeting in person (see Note-Taking Evidence Guide).*

Additional Data for Your Collection:

- Review all medical documents, including diagnostic work.
- Physician: Highlight all related diagnostic write ups.
- Clinical Psychologist: Feature all instructional recommendations.
- Neurological Testing: Include DSM IV or diagnosis like ADHD
- Speech and Language: Attach all suggested therapies.
- Other:

Notes:

Note-taking/Evidence Guide:

Physician/Therapist/Services Diagnosis: DSM (official) Recommendations:

_____   _____

_____   _____

_____   _____

_____   _____

_____   _____

_____   _____

_____   _____

_____   _____

_____   _____

Additional notes and comments:

_____

_____

_____

_____

_____

_____

Present Levels of Performance Checklist

DISABILITY(S):

_____

_____

_____

_____

Summary (write a statement highlighting your child's current levels of performance, related to medical diagnosis, school performance, and evaluations):

_____

_____

Academic/General Education performance (reading/writing/math/other):

What works?

_____

_____

_____

_____

What are her/his challenges?

_____

_____

_____

_____

Social/Emotional (Peer and adult relationships, expressive and receptive language, sense of self-worth, emotional state of mind at school):

_____

_____

_____

_____

What works?

_____

_____

_____

_____

What are her/his challenges?

_____

_____

_____

_____

Cognitive (intelligence): Formal assessments as measured by WISC/WIAT and other evaluations

WISC (Ability):   Score Comments:

Verbal Comprehension   ____   _____

Perceptual Reasoning   ____   _____

Processing Speed   ____   _____

Working Memory   ____   _____

Strengths within the cognitive assessments:

_____

_____

_____

_____

Challenges as evaluated:

_____

_____

_____

_____

WIAT/WJR (Achievement):   Score   Comments:

Reading   Basic___ Fluency___ Comp___   _____

Math   Calc___ Reasoning___ Prob___   _____

Written Language   ___ ___   _____

Listening   ___ ___   _____

Oral Expression   ___ ___   _____

Strengths within the assessments:

_____

_____

_____

Challenges within the assessments:

_____

_____

Physical: Health, wellness, activities:

_____

_____

_____

_____

Interests (Outside of school): "Bridging" activities to his/her success at school

_____

_____

_____

_____

Additional Information:

_____

_____

_____

_____

For those with a current IEP:

Annual Goals:	Measured by:	Expected Outcome	Current Data/Present Levels:
_____	_____	_____	_____
_____	_____	_____	_____
_____	_____	_____	_____
_____	_____	_____	_____

Success since last IEP meeting:

_____

_____

Concerns since last IEP meeting:

_____

_____

Getting Started: Evidence Based

Both the Section 504 and IEP processes require a team decision to determine if there appears to be a significant impact between your child's disability and his/her achievement in school. **Nevertheless, your primary purpose is to move the discussion from a subjective one to an objective, evidence-based discussion**. This is a two-step process. With a new referral, your focus is to assure the team mutually understands the disability in question and secondly, sees a significant impact within the present levels. Do not worry about which level of support, 504 plan or IEP, at this point in time.

For New Referrals:

Prepare an email requesting a meeting with the following information:

Statement of request: "*I am requesting a "focus of concern" meeting as soon as possible to address my child's challenges at school*".

- ***If your child has an established disability or diagnosis:***

"*At that time, we can focus on the impact [disability] has on his/her overall performance.*"

Optional statement to add: "*We are exploring the possibility of support through*:

Section 504 Plan (General Education accommodation plan)

IEP (Specially Designed Instruction)".

- ***If your child does not have an established disability or diagnosis:***

"*At that time, we can focus on my son's current present levels of performance compared to his/her peers within the context of ...*" [add the specific areas of concern]:

☐ Academic ☐ Behavior ☐ Cognitive ☐ Communication ☐ Emotional ☐ Physical ☐ Social

Statement of evidence: "*Specifically, we will address the challenges my child experiences at school and it would be most helpful if you had the following items at the meeting to support our discussion and ideally, guide our decisions*". [If the team does not have these items, you will. It puts you in the position of control.]

- Sample classroom work (most recent samples of writing, etc.)
- Homework and assignments (graded projects, samples)
- Assessments and testing (WASL, other assessments, class tests)
- Report Cards (most recent through all grades)
- Emails written between school and home highlighting concerns

Send copies to your child's teacher and principal. The decision on what specific plan of action may best be decided at the meeting, unless you are clear on the significance of the impact and the specific accommodations and services needed.

Beginning the Process: Moving Forward

STEP ONE:

The school-based team [i.e.; Student Study Team/MDT/Guidance Team] decides if there is enough evidence to warrant an evaluation; addressing the following question:

> *Does the disability previously identified present a significant impact on learning or does there appear to be a suspected disability impacting learning?*

Typically, the team has 25 school days* to address this question from the day you brought it to their attention as a "focus of concern." An email or signed letter of request is enough to get the process moving. **Ask to be invited to this meeting for it is not always a given that parents attend this initial discussion.**

* In some states, the 25 school day period falls within the federal 60 school day calendar.

The three possible outcomes from this initial meeting will be: Evaluate, 504 Plan, or no change

STEP TWO:

"Yes" Move to Evaluation

> The team agrees to move forward with the Evaluation; you will immediately be asked to sign documents asking for your permission to evaluate your child. The process will take no more than 60 days from your initial "focus of concern" to completion of the formal evaluation.
>
> As a result, the team has another 35 days (60 days in all from referral to evaluation to decision) to assess, test, and collect data to determine if there is a relationship between a suspected disability and your child's learning; this is the formal Evaluation segment of the IEP process.

"No" No formal Evaluation; move to Section 504 Plan

> The team <u>agrees</u> that there is a connection between an identified disability or a suspected disability and learning; however, the members believe that the most appropriate intervention would be through a Section 504 Plan. [*Another meeting to follow*].
>
> As a result, the team will likely meet within a reasonable period of time and establish accommodations addressing the suspected disability and your child's learning as part of the General Education program. The Section 504 document developed will require an annual meeting for review.

"No" No change

> The team does <u>not agree</u> that there is a connection and believes that the most appropriate intervention would be to "stay the course" and continue to serve your child through General Education support without accommodations (504 Plan) or the possibility of an IEP (specially designed instruction). [*You have options if you are not satisfied with this response*].
>
> <u>Response to Intervention (RTI) Option</u>: Within the Federal update guiding Special Education law, IDEA 2004, the RTI model encourages states and districts to implement a

school-wide intervention approach to identifying intervention for all students who are not succeeding within the General Education program. If your child is not achieving at the expected level of his or her peers, and does not access either a 504 Plan or an IEP, then you will be working with your child's teacher and principal within the school's Response to Intervention program [if it exists]. This may get a bit "fuzzy" for each school and/or district has created its own intervention model; there are no federal guidelines and requirements.

General Comments: All or Nothing and The Inconvenient Truth!

When you move forward with a "focus of concern" and the formal Evaluation process, it may feel like you are entering another world; similar to Dorothy moving through the Land of Oz to reach the Emerald City. You may experience hurdles and challenges along the way, as if you are trying to visit the Wizard. However, your intent is to "lift the curtain" and move the conversation about your child's learning from subjective to **objective**, from emotions to **facts**. It is critical that in IEP and 504 Plan considerations, evaluations and documentation guide the team discussion. By following the Note Taking/Evidence Guide, you will be leading the process toward an evidence-based intervention discussion; and the school will have no other choice then to follow your lead!

When learning challenges are matched with behavioral issues, such that the behavior causes a distraction to teaching and learning, teachers and staff are often the first ones to initiate the referral and call on the parents to request an Evaluation. If your child is highly inconvenient, then everyone is calling out the need for a 504 Plan or an IEP. For example, if a disability like ADHD or Autism has a behavior related symptom, which is a distraction within the class, then the staff makes a compelling case for a 504 or IEP plan (significant impact). Sometimes, staff members take it farther by guiding the conversation with questions: "Have you considered medication?" or "Does your son see a therapist?"

However, this may not be the case in your situation for numbers of parents find accessing both IEP and 504 Plan support fairly challenging. Even more so, through years of advocacy addressing Section 504 Plans, this process tends to present the most difficult challenge for parents especially when there may be conflicting agendas, opinions, or evidence at the core. For example, when behavior is not an issue, a student who is earning C's or D's in class or barely passing state assessment exams, the team will often make the case that the impact is mild or moderate, not enough for a 504 accommodation nor an IEP. This is why we have to go back to the three guiding questions in every case:

1. Is there an established disability or diagnosis? Or a suspected diagnosis or disability?
2. What impact does this disability or diagnosis have on my son or daughter's school experience including academic, social, emotional, or behavior considerations?
3. Finally, when considering interventions, if we have established mutual understanding related to #1 and #2 above, how would Specially Designed Instruction through an IEP or accommodations via a Section 504 Plan be appropriate?

Important to note, often the C or D student may be causing absolute chaos at home, possibly in a deep depression, or losing sleep as a result of the disability. It is only when the school sees F grades that many teachers deem the impact as significant, unless behavior presents an impact on teaching and learning. Frequently, it's the male student with ADHD, the one who can't sit still in class, who gets 504/IEP support, while the female student with ADD, the one who has reverted to her own internal world within her notebook, possibly overlooked as "being spacey" or given another personality trait, like "flighty", does not warrant support for her challenges are not inconvenient. Consider the facts:

Male students with special needs are more than twice as likely as females to receive special services through an Individualized Education Plan (IEP). In 2007, 42 percent of boys with special needs in kindergarten through third grade had an IEP, compared with seventeen percent of girls with special needs in the same grades. (Child Trends 2014)

Trumping an Agenda with Data

I frequently receive phone calls from concerned parents stating their child did not qualify for a Section 504 Plan or an IEP; this can be frustrating when there is clear evidence that a relationship exists between a disability and its negative impact on learning. In these situations, when the burden of proof shifts from teachers and staff to the parent's side of the table, this can feel like an intimidating task if a parent is not prepared. However, by following the strategies presented within the "Insider's Guide", you are up for the challenge. By trumping the report card, or any other single form of assessment, which does not reflect the "big picture" of your child's challenges at school, one needs to establish a counter-punch through additional data collected to offset non-qualifying agendas: Here are two ways to explore:

1. Get a diagnosis from a physician or licensed clinician in writing. It is very difficult for teachers and other non-physicians to diminish a medical evaluation especially if the referring physician or therapist cites the DSM IV or V reference guide. This becomes most evident in cases where anxiety, stress-symptoms, and other social-emotional conditions take its toll. Also, within the context of ADD/ADHD, which continues to be on the rise each year, Executive Functioning related disorders may be identified by clinicians in conjunction with attention-related disabilities; for many students, EF symptoms present a pronounced impact on learning. Once the diagnosis is established, a review of classwork, homework, assignments, and course-related tests, in addition to formal assessments, would likely demonstrate the impact if this is truly the case*.

* The law and related policies are clear; just because a child has a disability or a diagnosis, a 504 Plan or an IEP are not guaranteed; impact guides the decision. Also, the law and state guidelines require more than one assessment for identification.

2. Find an assessment tool which moves the conversation from perception to evaluation. This also may be evident when addressing ADD/ADHD related issues, especially when the intervention team presents the connection between behavior and learning simply as a matter of motivation, laziness, or a general lack of parental support at home. For issues related to your child's emotional state, the BASC II is an excellent assessment tool to establish a baseline addressing behavior, emotional state of mind, and other related issues through teacher, parent, and student-self assessment. When addressing the impact of ADD/ADHD or Autism, often processing related issues are at the core of the behaviors demonstrated. In these situations, the WISC IV is an outstanding evaluation tool which addresses processing and its relationship to learning specifically, when taking in account the four WISC sub-tests mentioned:

- Verbal comprehension: This is the ability to process verbal, language-based information. Typical classroom instruction is primarily auditory, through teacher talks and lectures. This is how we relate to the world - through verbal comprehension. We are a "listen up," "let's talk it over," "do you hear me?" society. Students with language processing issues often score lower in this area of the IQ test process and on the other side of the coin, students who present themselves well, with excellent conversation/negotiation skills, often demonstrate higher scores on this subtest of the WISC.

- <u>Perceptual Reasoning</u>: This is the ability to process non-verbal information, in a written/block design format. This is best described as the "do you see what I am talking about?" type of thinking; when the person visualizes the new ideas. Students who excel with perceptual reasoning-like activities are hands-on types, the Lego crowd, and are often kids who need to see it before understanding. This may be one of the subtle areas of the evaluation process, because perceptual reasoning is not emphasized in the classroom like language based verbal comprehension activities.

- <u>Working Memory</u>: This is the ability to process multiple steps at once; juggling a multiple bits of information at the same time. Often this is where math becomes an issue. Think of this as the amount of information someone can handle at one time. Often students with issues here have difficulty with multi-step directions, lists of things, and remembering a complex process. For these students, learning may require repetitious practice before things get "locked in." ADD/ADHD students often score low in this area.

- <u>Processing Speed</u>: This is the ability to work and process information quickly; some students need more thinking time to truly understand and make connections to learning. Most often, this is an issue when students need additional time to work things out. Often very intelligent kids require more time to "get it" and within the classroom setting, by the time the student understands the presented concepts, the class has already moved on to new ideas and new lessons. Many kids on the Autism Spectrum demonstrate a significant gap between Processing Speed scores and other assessments.

Take note: it is essential that you review the subtests within the WISC in contrast to the full scale score. For example, an average student may score between 90 and 110 on an IQ battery on the full scale, but there are significant impacts on learning when one or more of the indexes (or sub-tests) are inconsistent with the full scale, especially if there's a 15-20 point difference or differential. This causes the full scale to be an invalid measurement.

WISC Full Scale IQ = 110 (high average)

- Verbal = 121
- Perceptual= 102
- Working Memory= 89
- Processing=105

 In the case above, the student's full scale IQ is average, not an issue or concern if he or she is earning A's – D's on report cards, while further discovery highlights the working memory score as 32 points below the verbal comprehension score of 121. This student functions within the "superior range" with a 121 Verbal IQ but struggles with the amount of new information at one time as demonstrated in the Working Memory subtest. She may appear to be highly intelligent, due to the 121 Verbal score, and at the same time, fails her classes. She may be perceived by teachers as not applying herself or lazy, when it may be a matter of processing, as demonstrated in the 89 Working Memory or 105 Processing Speed sub-tests.

The use of a WISC, like most formal assessment tools, takes the discussion from generalizations such as: "just not trying enough...lazy...unmotivated" to specific information highlighting ability and/or achievement; moving from subjective to objective. As an Education Advocate, the WISC IQ evaluation tool provides one of the most valuable information tools possible for it highlights processing and related issues and its impact on learning. Again, as your child's advocate, you need to build a case moving from perception to evaluation. The information found within the WISC is your ace in the hole; in most cases, processing is everything - or at least the tip of the iceberg.

Sample Evaluation Tools:

Academic (cognitive intelligence, processing)

- WISC III/IV (Wechsler Intelligence Scale for Children): The standard intelligence test which highlights processing through pattern analysis of the sub-tests; excellent reference complimenting additional tests, assessments, and data.

- CTONI (Comprehensive Test of Nonverbal Intelligence): An alternative intelligence test with a non-verbal perspective. This test is best for use with students who have language related issues like Autism, Speech and Language, ESL.

- DAS (Differentiated Ability Scales): This cognitive assessment for kids from 2.5 years old features diagnostic subtests measuring a variety of cognitive abilities including verbal and visual working memory, immediate and delayed recall, visual recognition and matching, processing and naming speed, phonological processing, and understanding of basic number concepts.

Achievement (academic performance)

- WIAT/WJR III (Wechsler Individual Achievement Test/Woodcock Johnson): The standard achievement tests featuring achievement in core subjects including reading, math, and written expression. It is broken into sub-tests for each content area.

- Kaufman Test of Educational Achievement (KTEA): Covers many of the same criteria within the WIAT and WJR, however, it may take less time.

Behavior:

- Connors Continuous Performance Test is an assessment tool addressing attention and related skill sets often associated with ADD/ADHD assessments.

- TOVA (Test of Variables of Attention): Another attention related test administered by schools and within clinical settings.

- BASC 2 (Behavior Assessment System for Children): The standard elements include behaviors which are keeping the student from success, assessment tool addressing a wide range of issues including aggression, antecedents/causes of the behavior, functional purpose of the anxiety, depression, and social skills based upon parent, teacher, and a child's self-assessment.

Language Skills:

- CELF (Clinical Evaluation of Language Fundamentals): Another standard evaluation tool highlighting reading, language expression, receptive language and written language, most notably in the Speech and Language evaluation process. Excellent tool for higher functioning students with autism or Asperger syndrome, as well as students with receptive or expressive language concerns. Excellent assessment as a follow-up to WISC or achievement tests.

Physical (balance, coordination, spatial and strength)

- Sensory Integration and Praxis Test: This assessment tool is the with an IEP would benefit primarily related to sensory, tactile, kinesthetic, motor related issues and it is often applied to an OT evaluation, and assists in number of situations including Autism Spectrum assessments.

Social, Functional, and Adaptive Life Skills:

- Vineland 2 (Vineland Adaptive Behavior Scales): An assessment tool addressing personal and social skills needed for everyday living; helps identify social skills related to intellectual disability or other disorder such as autism, Asperger syndrome and developmental delays.

Social and Emotional Development of Infants and Toddlers:

- BITSEA (The Brief Infant-Toddler Social and Emotional Assessment): Another standard assessment tool specifically designed for children up to 36 months addressing a wide range of social and emotional skills i.e.; social skills, language, and developmental delays.

When to Seek the Guidance of an Expert: Advocate, Attorney, or Ombudsman?

While it's essential to create a strategic plan before going in to an IEP/504 meeting, there will be times when you will feel overwhelmed and/or under-prepared; it goes with the territory until you do this work hundreds of times. Till then, it's in your child's best interest to call for assistance every now and then. In fact, if you are following along with the "Insider's Guide" to this point, you are so far ahead of the game! However, due to the complexity of your child's needs, and the lack of transparency within the IEP or 504 process, this is one of those times it can be invaluable to seek outside assistance for perspective. While the "Insider's Guide" provides the foundation for your step-by-step planning, reviewing your strategy with a professional will help tap into another's expertise to secure your advocacy position with confidence. Knowing you are on-target will always be a valuable element of your game plan for you will be working within a well-entrenched system and its' players are often highly skilled in the negotiation process*.

Sure, I would prefer to call it a "collaborative experience", and when the IEP and 504 Plan processes resemble transparency and genuine partnership, it really can be collaborative and in fact, an inspiration due to the creativity and ingenuity developed when people are working together as a team.

Advocates: Many of us are educators and the benefit of working with an experienced Advocate may be founded upon his or her experience as an "insider"; knowing the culture of schools from a teaching and administration perspective provides invaluable insight for parents as well as team members sitting across the table. As a result, we are able to support the process as a respected member of the team rather than being perceived as an "outsider" and worse, an adversary.

Knowledgeable Advocates understand curriculum, instruction, special education law, and most notably, kids!

Attorneys: When you are needing a legal expert on matters related to Special Education, an experienced attorney is a most valued resource. Personally, I refer to my legal colleagues frequently, especially when cases cross the threshold within Due Process. I tend to think of an attorney as follows: When gardening, I use a variety of tools: rakes, shovels, hoes, and shears. However, when I am doing large hardscape work, none of these tools do the job and a backhoe or tractor will only get the job done. Same for special needs support, there are times when an experienced Advocate will not be enough to get the job done due to the complexity of the legal system and the services of an attorney are needed. From my perspective, attorneys are the backhoes of special education!

Ombudsmen: Throughout country, many school districts and states have figured out that the Special Education business is fairly complex for most parents. As a result, many have established Ombudsmen support services to level the playing the field. Once again, I access our state Ombudsman services all the time, especially, when I am needing in-depth information related to ever-changing laws and new guidelines. I highly recommend their services if available in your region. However, most Ombudsmen are unable to attend meetings.

Are You Shooting from the Hip or Working From Script?

I highly recommend parents create 3x5 script cards so your intention, strategy, and recall of data doesn't get lost in the heat of the moment at these meetings. The intensity of the process may cause parents to lose focus; sometimes our emotions get the best (or the worst) of us. The most critical talking points will always be the following:

1. Is there an established disability or diagnosis? Or a suspected diagnosis or disability?

2. What impact does this disability or diagnosis have on my son or daughter's school experience including academic, social, emotional, or behavior considerations?
   a. Review the most essential information from your Note Taking / Evidence Guide or the IEP/504 Checklist.
   b. Have copies of the Evaluations with you.
   c. Find a copy of the DSM IV/V (the official diagnosis) worksheet online.

3. Finally, when considering interventions, if we have established mutual understanding related to #1 and #2 above, how would Specially Designed Instruction through an IEP or Section 504 Plan Accommodations be appropriate?

<u>IEP/504 Planning Checklist</u>:

❏   General Education/Classroom Accommodations: *previously established; IEP or 504*

❏   Disability/Diagnosis: *See Evaluations from Clinicians*

- Specific Learning Disability: _____   (example: reading)
- Health Impairment/Other: _____   (example: ADHD)
- Copy of the diagnostic DSM (including typical symptoms)

❏   Data (include copies of the following):

- IQ and Achievement Evaluations (formal evaluations with scores)
    - WISC (IQ):   Verbal ____   Perceptual ____
        - Working Memory ____   Processing Speed ____
    - WIAT: Oral Expression ____   Listening ____
        - Written Expression ____   Basic Reading ____
        - Reading Comprehension ___   Math Calculation ____
        - Math Reasoning ____   other: _____
- Medical diagnostic work: neurological report, speech, clinical psychologist
- Academic Assessment results: ITBS, Reading Inventory, Dibbles
- Report Cards: grades and teacher comments stating areas of concern
- Emails: teacher's areas of concern or previous accommodations
- Discipline Records: suspensions, referrals, time-outs
- Proposed or past IEP, 504 plan, or evaluation results: *ask for documents a couple days before the meeting; this allows you to preview what's to come.*

❏   List of Previous Accommodations and Support Services:

<u>Within the Classroom</u>:

Activity:	Purpose:	Dates: Impact: *example*
After school reading	Increase reading fluency 9/05-	Still below grade

_____

_____

_____

_____

_____

_____

_____

Within a "pullout" program or outside of class:

Activity: Purpose: Dates: Impact: *example*

After school reading   Increase reading fluency 9/05-   Still below grade

_____

_____

_____

After or Before School:

_____

_____

_____

Parent Supported Services (academic):

_____

_____

Other services or support:

_____

_____

For Students with a current or previous IEP:

❐ List the specific areas with Specially Designed Instruction:

Reading __ Math __ Written Language __ Communication __ Social Skills__ Behavior__ OT/PT__

Annual Goals: Measured by: Expected Outcome   Current Data / Present Levels:

_____   _____ _____   _____

_____   _____ _____   _____

_____   _____ _____   _____

_____   _____ _____   _____

_____   _____ _____   _____

_____   _____ _____   _____

During the Meeting:

Stay the Course and Other Insights

A few things to know upfront: Key members of the team (school psychologist, special education teacher, your child's teacher, and/or an administrator) have probably met before the scheduled Student Study Team, 504, IEP, or Evaluation meeting. They will have developed a specific outcome they are striving for, and an agenda will have been pre-determined without your participation. As a result, if you are not on the same page as the team, you may be looking at an uphill battle. This is why you want to communicate with all teachers and staff beforehand and establish understanding prior to the meeting; this may include email documentation from previous conversations.

If the meeting is a follow-up to a guidance meeting, or following the initial IEP meeting, then evaluation tests, related assessments, or IEP/504 proposals should be made available prior to the actual meeting; you should ask for copies to be sent to you beforehand (at least 48 hours in advance); allowing you the opportunity to read and review draft documents.

The standard procedure would be to read the materials verbatim during the meeting which takes up valuable discussion time. This can be most frustrating for parents who take time off from work and listen to others read documents that can be read at home. Furthermore, if the IEP and 504 related proposals are not clearly understood by the common person on the street, and require an education interpreter, then in most cases, they are poorly written.

Everything is negotiable; there are few set-in-concrete solutions to learning issues. The same diagnosis with similar achievement patterns may be handled differently at each school, within the district, as well as within the state; in many situations, it's a matter of negotiating through a push-pull process. Under best conditions, it's a collaborative process supported by creativity, innovation, and ingenuity. However it plays out, every IEP and 504 Plan takes on a different look based upon the composition of those engaged in the process. Even though one can read online or hear from a friend what their child's IEP or 504 may look like, keep mind, no two documents look the same!

Many IEP and 504 teams anticipate parents will go along with their decisions; most parents do. Nevertheless, as an Education Advocate since 1998, and a school administrator since 1988, I have seen extraordinary variations on services, accommodations and team decisions. It is our role through advocacy to create individualized plans rather than cookie cutter interventions. In fact, within the IEP process alone, the team always has the "professional judgment" option as the basis for qualification for Special Education services, by-passing typical discrepancy guidelines and making a team decision based upon what is appropriate and within reason. Professional judgment, though not the preferred decision process for qualifying for an IEP (from the school district perspective), takes the conversation from the discrepancy model to an individual needs discussion. In fact, I have seen many professional judgment based IEP plans created due to a student's behavior alone, when his or her behavior is a nuisance and a severe distraction to the learning process. Through a round of BASC behavior scales distributed amongst teachers and a few observations by the School Psychologist, students can easily qualify for an IEP if there happens to be strong agenda to do so. Again, it's in your child's best interest to try to flush out the agenda prior to meeting with staff.

Ready, Set, Go ...

If you followed the suggestions laid out within the "Insider's Guide", did your homework, and know your child from an educator's perspective, then you are ready for the meetings. You don't need to be an expert on curriculum nor be up to speed on instructional strategies; just know, your understanding of your child alone from the "Insider's Guide" lens, puts you in an extraordinary position. This will allow you to focus more on the process and maintain attention on your specific outcome instead of feeling overwhelmed by information and caught off guard by emotions (yours).

Trust me on this: you will be a true trailblazer by following the strategies suggested. You will be the most focused, prepared, and knowledgeable person in the room. Your child will be well represented by you, and your advocacy skills will be rewarded for your efforts. Finally, you are making your case based upon the following strategy:

- Know the diagnosis and make sure there is mutual understanding within the team before moving forward with additional discussion.
- Establish a fact-based, evaluation-supported, classroom evidence connection between the disability and the present levels of performance. No stone left unturned! Again, this needs to be a mutually understood perspective and you should not move in to interventions until there are common grounds of understanding related to the impact of the disability or diagnosis.
- Either accommodations (504 plans) and specially designed instruction (IEP) will be developed in support of your child once the team has successfully moved through steps 1 and 2.*
- Also know, you are your child's parent-advocate, and possibly, in the best position to understand the nature of your son or daughter. Let the staff be the curriculum and instruction experts. And if you feel their expertise is lacking, you may want to run this by an Advocate for additional insights and perspective.

* 504 teams may require YOU to present accommodations

Bring the Three F's: Food, Fotos, and Facts

More often than you would imagine, the team probably met before the meeting and determined a strategic outcome before you walk in the door; hearts and minds may already be locked in to a pre-determined path and the meeting may just be a formality to some of the team members. There are ways you can set a tone working toward mutual understanding: food and photos break the ice.

The gesture of bringing food goes far by expressing both thoughtfulness and appreciation; food around a table establishes a collaborative tone (breaking bread) and often breaks the tension within adversarial relations, if any have developed prior to the meeting. From my experience, chocolate and cookies work well in the afternoon sessions and beverages may be best for the mornings.

As for photos, this technique allows the team to remain focused and present with your child's needs, when the tendency is often to go one-size-fits all and lose touch of your child's gifts, strengths, and challenges. The use of a large 8x10 portrait serves two purposes:

First, it allows those who don't know your child opportunity to put a face with a name.

Secondly, it may minimize the impact of those who really don't know your child within the conversation, and allows you opportunity to establish yourself as your child's best advocate. Since you are working from the heart, all other members of the team take a supplemental position to an informed and loving parent.

Finally, by bringing the facts with you, with documentation within arm's reach, you will be able to offset the preconceived notions with hard-core evidence. It keeps everyone in check when you are informed! Most members of the team will likely shoot from the hip, whereas a data-driven perspective is hard to argue with.

Let the Team's Facilitator Establish his/her Direction

Always let the meeting facilitator open the meeting and set an agenda. You are a guest within their home, and it's best to let the process first unfold. If the facilitator immediately establishes the agenda with the point of view, "What is NOT working for your child?" Find a seamless moment to assert your position: "Let's address my child's strengths first before we address her shortfalls." Establishing present levels of performance with his or her strengths sets the right tone.

If there are no specific outcomes or a purpose of the meeting stated, clarify and restate your opening position/intention:

> *"By the end of today's meeting, we/I intend on walking out with*:

IEP-related:

- Initial IEP: "*Agreement that my son/daughter will be evaluated for an IEP and the evaluation process will be initiated as soon as possible.*"
- Initial IEP (after evaluations): "*An understanding how my son/daughter qualified for an IEP with specially designed instruction to be developed as soon as possible.*"
- Initial IEP (after IEP qualification): "*Clearly designed goals, objectives, and related support services directly aligned with his/her disability to include measurable ways of establishing his/her growth, so we can easily monitor his/her progress.*"
- Established IEP (already in place): "*Revised goals, objectives, and related support services directly aligned with his/her current levels of performance and disability. An addendum (adjustments) needs to be developed, because she is not succeeding in school with her current IEP in place.*"

"A 504 plan" related [be prepared to present accommodations]

- Initial 504: "*A plan with appropriate accommodations directly aligned with my daughter's disability to level the playing field so she can succeed. She has a number of challenges impacting her performance at school. And a 504 Plan will make a big difference.*"
- Established 504: "*Update the plan with additional accommodations. She is continuing to struggle due to the disability, and the previous plan was not effective.*"

Notes:

Bring a Friend, Spouse, or Guest to Take Notes and Chart Decisions

It can be a three-ring challenge to juggle the information being exchanged, maintaining emotional balance, and taking notes at the same time. A note-taker is always an asset (See Meeting Worksheet). If your note-taker is also skilled at charts, it is also effective to create a decision making chart (see sample later in the guidebook) to hold the meeting tighter toward an action-oriented session. In addition, if there is an official note-taker, ask for copies of as well. Also, have a seating chart ready to pass around so you know their names, positions, and connection to your child, rather than feeling completely out of the loop. The use of this seating chart will <u>absolutely</u> cause a major shift in the meeting; it will present you as one who is informed and wants to continue to be:

"Since I am the one person who really doesn't know everyone, if you would please complete this chart as we go around, it would be most helpful, especially if I am needing to follow up today's meeting with a conversation or update. Thank you."

Name/Role: How you know my child?   Name/Role: How you know my child?   Name/Role: How you know my child?

Name/Role: How you know my child?   Name/Role: How you know my child?   Name/Role: How you know my child?

Notes:

<u>Meeting Worksheet: IEP 504 Plan</u>

Attending:

_____   _____   _____   _____   _____

_____   _____   _____   _____   _____

Purpose of meeting: Initial IEP/504   Annual IEP/504 IEP/504 Addendum   Evaluation

DISABILITY(S):

_____

_____

Summary (write a statement highlighting child's current levels of performance, related to medical diagnosis, school performance, and evaluations):

Academic/General Education performance (reading/writing/math/other):

- What works?

_____

_____

_____

- What are her/his challenges?

_____

_____

_____

Social/Emotional (peer and adult relationships, expressive and receptive language, sense of self-worth, emotional state of mind at school)

- What works?

_____

_____

_____

- What are his/her challenges?

_____

_____

_____

Cognitive (intelligence): Formal assessments as measured by WISC or other evaluation tools

WISC (Ability):   Score   Comments:

      Verbal Comprehension ____   _____
      Perceptual Reasoning ____   _____
      Processing Speed   ____   _____
      Working Memory   ____   _____

- Strengths within the cognitive assessments:

_____

_____

_____

- Challenges as evaluated:

_____

_____

_____

WIAT/WJR (Achievement):   Score   Comments:

      Reading   ___ ___ ___   _____
      Math   ___ ___ ___   _____
      Written Language ___ ___   _____
      Listening   ___ ___   _____
      Oral Language   ___ ___   _____

- Strengths within the assessments:

_____

_____

_____

- Challenges within the assessments:

_____

_____

_____

_____

_____

Physical: Health, wellness, activities

_____

_____

_____

Interests (Outside of school): "Bridging" activities to his/her success at school

_____

_____

_____

Accommodations within General Education setting currently in place:

Accommodation:	Facilitator:	Purpose:
Seating, adjusted assignments	_Teachers_	_Increase focus_

_____

_____

_____

_____

_____

Specially Designed Instruction (IEP) currently in place:

SDI:	Facilitated By:	Purpose/Goal:	Measured by:
Study skills class, Teachers	_Increase reading_	_4th grade level_	_Brigance Test_

_____

_____

_____

_____

_____

Accommodations within General Education setting PROPOSED:

Accommodation: Facilitator: Purpose:

Seating, adjusted assignments   *Teachers*   *Increase focus*

_____

_____

_____

_____

_____

Specially Designed Instruction (IEP) PROPOSED:

SDI: Facilitated By: Purpose/Goal: Measured by:

Study skills class, Teachers   *Increase reading*   *4th grade level*   *Brigance Test*

_____

_____

_____

_____

_____

_____

Next Meeting:

Date: Purpose of Meeting   Information/Resources Needed for Meeting:

Oct. 28   *Review behavior plans*   *Suspensions, class discipline, referrals*

_____   _____   _____

_____   _____   _____

Notes:

STEP ONE: Remind team of the disability and the typical symptoms:

Distribute the disability DSM IV/V, medical diagnosis, or related documents if the team continues to question the validity of the disability. You may need to stay put at this step before moving forward. If you continue to have backlash from the team, or if there are questions about the diagnosis, your information will be most valuable. Coming to a mutual understanding, related to the disability or diagnosis, provides the essential foundation for upcoming discussion. This may present itself as a point of contention and may require an **Independent Education Evaluation** (IEE: See Procedural Safeguards) afterwards if you and the team cannot come to mutual understanding.

STEP TWO: Establish Present Levels of Performance:

A well-developed present levels, including strengths, diagnosis-based disabilities, and classroom-based performance, will set the stage for further discussion. Also, make sure the conversation addresses current interventions and their impact highlighting evidence and data.

Follow the present levels worksheet from the earlier section of the guidebook. Make sure the team sees your child "as is" before moving into a discussion about qualifying, services and accommodations. This is a valuable piece to highlight visually on a chart; a "portrait" of your child!

STEP THREE: Ask questions when something doesn't make sense:

The feeling that you are bombarded with too much information is quite common, and in fact, it is the honest-to-goodness truth. In addition, the team members often use educational jargon which is not familiar to most parents. So whenever you are in a position of uncertainty, ask for clarification and seek out examples for understanding. For this reason, many parents record the meetings (with prior notice) to assure everything presented was well understood.

STEP FOUR: Ask for accommodations, resources, and decisions to be written on a whiteboard or chart paper:

The meetings tend to be an endless stream of talk; creating a running record of mutually agreed-upon decisions will be most valuable for follow-up meetings.   The best way to manage the information is as follows: Diagnosis, Present Levels, Accommodations/SDI, and written in common language understood by parents and anyone else outside of the educational community: All interventions & accommodations need to pass THE STRANGER TEST: would anyone off the street be able to understand the document? If not, **re-write till you get it right!**

Sample Chart: 504 Plan

Disability	Present Levels	Accommodation	Who/When?	Purpose
ADHD:	*Organ. & planning*	*Daily review, planner*	*Teachers/daily*	*Enhance Com.*

Sample Chart: Specific IEP Plan of Action

GOAL(S): The specific learning target:	Moving From:	Moving To:	Measured By:
Reading: Increasing Comprehension	*5th grade level*	*6th grade level*	*STAR Reading*

ACCOMMODATIONS: What Can They Look Like?

Due to the nature of 504 Plans being vague and less specific, compared to IEP related goals, the following guidelines will assist as you are working with the team. Do consider that each school and district tends to place their own spin on a 504 document so it's most important that the following guidelines are considered, however, you may feel pressure to keep accommodations general and non-specific:

- The document makes sense to you, your child, and anyone responsible for implementation
- The purpose of the 504 Plan needs to be spelled out including:
    - Disability as defined by a licensed clinician.
    - Impact as it presents itself within class, school, and home; more specific information the better!
- As far as accommodations, the following guidelines are important considerations:
    - What will the accommodation look like?
    - When will it be available?
    - Who will implement the accommodation?
    - What is the purpose of this accommodation?*
    - How will the team know it is working? Or not?*

* Due to the lack of specific forms, or guidelines at the state and federal level, it would be most fortunate and highly unusual to have these elements addressed within a 504 Plan.

GOALS (for an IEP): Goldilocks and the Three Bears

In contrast to 504 Accommodations, IEP goals tend to follow guidelines and have a format to follow. From the parent's perspective, you might feel that the goals are way too general or the goals are too specific; you may feel like Goldilocks searching for the perfect bed until you get it "just right". And it may take a few IEP sessions or a whole different school, or district till you feel it works. It's the nature of the process to keep the goals manageable and not over-whelming to implement. However, Most Goals will be written as follows:

- <u>Measurable Annual Goals</u>; a description of how the school district will measure your student's progress towards meeting her/his annual goals, including <u>when</u> and <u>how often</u> the school district will provide periodic reports on the progress of your student.
- Typically, goals will be written with the following criteria: In order to be measurable, the goal statement should include the following:
    - a baseline ("from"),
    - a target ("to"),
    - and a unit of measure.
    - The baseline may be indicated in the present levels section of the IEP, as long as the unit of measure is consistent with the target.
- Good Example:
    - "Sue will increase her math computation skills in addition and subtraction moving from two-digit numbers with no regrouping to three digit numbers with regrouping as measured by STAR Math assessment system."
- Poor Example:

o   "Sue will increase her math computation skills at the 2nd grade level following the 3rd grade Common Core Standards". *How is it measured? And what specific skills are part of her Specially Designed Instruction?*

- See Annual Goal Quick Check: *This is a technical guide for IEP and Goal development; more for staff members responsible for developing an IEP. Informative.*

Quick Check

Measurable Annual Goals	Measurement Characteristics	Types of Criteria

Behavior
☐ addresses **individual** student need
☐ describes **observable** behavior
☐ **relates to** needs identified in student **data**
 	
Conditions
☐ describes circumstances or assistance **needed to perform** skill or behavior
 • clarifies what the performance of the skill should look like
 • circumstances
  o context
  o format
  o time
  o tools
 	
Criterion
☐ sets **mastery or proficiency level** for attainment of goal
☐ describes **progress** in a way that **can be measured**
☐ describes criterion to reflect grade level, rate, time, percentage or descriptive statement that is **understood by all** participants
☐ **relates** criterion **to current** student performance **data**
☐ describes **progress** expected **within a year**
	Specific
	 • the action, behavior, or skill to be measured
	 • tells what to measure and how to measure it
	
	Objective
	 • yields same result regardless of who measures it
	
	Quantifiable
	 • numerical or descriptive information that can be compared to previous data point
	
	Clear
	 • understandable by all involved, especially non-educators
	
	(Bateman, B. D. & Herr, C. M. (2003). *Writing Measurable IEP Goals and Objectives.* Verona, WI: Attainment.)
		Grade or Age Level
		 • an assigned numerical value to student performance
		 • must reference the source (test, etc.) and describe the skill it measures or the numerical value will not meet measurement requirements
		
		Rate
		 • the expected accuracy or frequency of a performance
		 • rate compares the number of correct behaviors, trials, or units of time with the total number
		
		Time
		 • time segment in which the behavior must be performed
		 • sets parameters for completing the performance
		 • used when speed of performance is important
		
		Percentage
		 • the number of correct responses compared to the total number of possible responses
		 • must define and be able to measure the whole
		
		Descriptive Statement
		 • description of the expected characteristics or quality of the final product/behavior in clear, objective language

Do's • use specific, clear information • target to student need • focus on student behavior • use quantifiable or descriptive information **Don'ts** • use vague information • copy curriculum without individualization • describe staff activities • use incomplete information		

Annual Goals–Make Them Measurable! Workshop–2005   1

<u>STEP FIVE:</u>   Ask about a <u>Prior Written Notice</u>

The Prior Written Notice document highlights proposed changes or refusals by the district. This serves as your formal documentation. Under 34 CFR §300.503(a), the school district must give you a written notice (information received in writing), whenever the school district*: The district has a "reasonable period of time" to provide.

1. Proposes to begin or change the identification, evaluation, or educational placement of your child or the provision of a free appropriate public education (FAPE) to your child; or
2. Refuses to begin or change the identification, evaluation, or educational placement of your child or the provision of FAPE to your child.
3. The school district must provide the notice in understandable language (34 CFR §300.503(c)).
4. Description of the action that the school district proposes or refuses to take.
5. Explanation of why the school district is proposing or refusing to take that action.

6. Description of each evaluation procedure, assessment, record, or report the school district used in deciding to propose or refuse the action.

7. Description of any other choices that the Individualized Education Program (IEP) Team considered and the reasons why those choices were rejected.

8. Description of other reasons why the school district proposed or refused the action:

* Part B PRIOR WRITTEN NOTICE U.S. Department of Education Model Form

STEP SIX: Establish specific follow-up dates and times, if plans are not finalized; create another chart to establish the next agend:

Meetings have a tendency to be a lot of talk and very little action. To assure each meeting is driven by a specific purpose and agenda, create a chart like the one below so you and the team will keep on-track and focused.

Date: Purpose of Meeting   Information Needed for Meeting:

Oct. 28 Review behavior plans   *Suspensions, class discipline, referrals*

_____   _____   _____

_____   _____   _____

If You Attend the Meeting with Another Person, an Advocate, or Specialist, Feel Comfortable to Seek a "Caucus"; Take a Breath!

Sometimes, walking out of the meeting for a strategic time-out is a good thing. This opportunity provides time to reflect and digest everything that has been proposed within the meeting. Just taking a breath of fresh air makes a difference. It also helps the district staff to rethink their position; which in many situations, can create a positive shift. A brief caucus can be exactly what's needed to move the negotiation process along. Notably, when a collaborative team moves from a stressful discussion to a momentary break of calm and ease, most often, the follow-up process projects revitalization and higher levels of problem solving. Pausing a moment from fast-forward allows everyone to re-charge and become more mindful of the tasks at hand.

Recommend the Meeting to be Rescheduled When You See:

- No one in attendance who directly knows your child.
- An Attorney representing the district.
- Comments about the "budget" or "union" as excuses.

If an attorney representing the district shows up, generally, your meeting is creating an issue requiring legal guidance. In most cases, if they bring an attorney, so should you! It would be in your best interest to reschedule and seek counsel. Secondly, most states have education codes in place assuring IEP membership. In WA State for example, state procedures highlight [392-172A 3095]

School Districts Must Assure the IEP Team Includes: *

- Parents
- Not less than one general education teacher
- Not less than one special education teacher or provider of related services
- A representative of the public agency who is qualified to provide or supervise specially designed instruction, who is knowledgeable about the general education curriculum, and availability of resources of the district
- At the discretion of the parent or district, anyone who has knowledge or special expertise regarding the student.
- The student, who should be invited when post-secondary goals and transition services after high school are being considered. I don't always recommend having the student attend the initial meeting, because the process may be contentious.

Also, budget issues and teacher union-related comments are never appropriate in limiting an appropriate IEP or 504 Plan accommodation; both are intervention plans of action based specifically on each student's needs. Though we all hear how "education is under-funded," specially designed instruction through your child's IEP drives the services, not budget limitations. For example, I have worked on numerous cases where students have access to highly expensive support including Instruction Assistants, Assistive Technology, or private education at the district's expense, at the same time the district is experiencing a budget crisis.

In most states, there are Safety Net programs allowing districts to apply for additional funding when an IEP moves into financial risk beyond basic funding and creates services requiring extraordinary expenses. Again, your child's IEP is supported by federal laws, which provide for FAPE (a free and appropriate public education), and the IEP as determined by the team. These extraordinary expenses should NEVER be a consideration within the context of an IEP and FAPE guidelines.

You also have the opportunity to waiver a member out of the meeting if you are needing to move forward with the meeting due to scheduling as long as essential members are available.

Notes:

After the Meeting:

Following Through

Most often, one meeting is never enough, because the typical IEP or 504 meeting only lasts 20-45 minutes. As I said before, since most parents just sign off on the proposal, there's usually no reason for additional time or meetings from the school's perspective. This is before they met you. So take your time and know you can always come back and address loose ends later. Keep in mind, follow-through is everything. In fact, by law, you can ask for a meeting anytime. However, one needs to be reasonable with this!

If you agree with the proposals as developed at the meeting, and you don't have copies of the official IEP or 504 documents in your possession when you walk out the door, make sure you follow the prescribed strategy below by restating your interpretation of the decisions agreed upon during the meeting.

If You Agree with the Decision

- Thank the person for the way the process was conducted via email, and ask for a copy of the official notes taken during the meeting and ask when the PRIOR WRITTEN NOTICE will be available.
- Highlight your understanding of specific decisions made at the meeting (see below) or provide a copy of your Meeting Worksheet (see earlier page).
- Ask for specific dates when the changes proposed will take place? Example:

Goals:	Services/Resources	Start date	Assessment	Evaluated by
Complete work	*Signed daily planner*	*Dec.30*	*Progress report*	*Jan.30*

If You Don't Agree with the Decision: Resolution Steps

This is a source of many client phone calls: I often hear from parents who feel they have been either backed into a corner, or just feel that the school already had a decision made up before the meeting took place. As a result, I spend a lot of time reviewing with folks the various options available. I strongly recommend that parents contact an Advocate, Attorney, or Ombudsmen prior to moving forward with one of the following dispute resolution resources:

Your options are defined within the **Procedural Safeguards**, *a handbook provided to you either at the beginning or the end of the meeting. As outlined, you have a number of options including:*

LEVEL ONE: Mediation is a voluntary process for parents and districts to meet to discuss their concerns with the help of a trained, neutral mediator. Mediation gives parents and districts the chance to resolve their special education concerns on their own. There is no cost for the mediation services. Most notably, both parties are encouraged to come to the table and seek resolution in good faith for this option to be successful for it is a voluntary process.

LEVEL TWO: Independent Educational Evaluation (IEE) of the student if the parent does not agree with the Evaluation and its findings.

- "You have the right to an IEE of your child at public expense if you disagree with an evaluation of your child conducted by your district, subject to the following conditions:
- If you request an IEE of your child at public expense, your school district must, within 15 calendar days of your request, **either**: (a) file a due process hearing request to show that its evaluation of your child is appropriate or that the evaluation of your child that you obtained did not meet the district's criteria; **or**, (b) agree to provide an IEE at public expense.
- If your school district requests a due process hearing and the final decision is that the district's evaluation of your child is appropriate, you still have the right to an IEE, but not at public expense.
- If you request an IEE of your child, your school district may ask why you object to the evaluation conducted by the district. However, the district may not require an explanation and may not unreasonably delay either providing the IEE of your child at public expense or filing a request for a due process hearing to defend the district's evaluation of your child.
- You are only entitled to one IEE of your child at public expense each time your school district conducts an evaluation of your child with which you disagree.

LEVEL THREE: Citizen Complaint is a written statement to your state or region Special Education agency alleging that a federal or state special education rule or law has been violated by the district within the 504 or IEP process. This is a valuable resource when a specific guideline with IDEA/FAPE (federal law) may have been poorly handled within the procedures governing both intervention plans. Examples may include:

- Failure to complete the Evaluation within the 60 day period
- Incomplete membership with IEP meetings, including parent participation issues

LEVEL FOUR: A Due Process hearing is a formal, legal proceeding conducted by an administrative law judge (ALJ). Parents and districts have a right to present and question witnesses, and to submit or challenge documents regarding the issues. This is highly adversarial; however, one of the benefits of the process is found within the mandatory *Resolution Meeting* required prior to going to court; this allows both parties opportunity to try to collaborate and create a resolution:

- A written request for a due process hearing is made by a parent or district relating to issues about the identification, evaluation, educational placement, or provision of Free Appropriate Public Education to a student. Requests must be made within—and allege violations that occurred not more than—**two years** before the date you knew or should have known about the allegation. Only an administrative law judge may allow an exception to the two-year time frame.

Seeking guidance of the Special Education Ombudsman (WA only)

- Office of the Education Ombudsman (Governor's Office):
  866-297-2597/ (no email)
- Office of the Superintendent of Public Instruction, Special Education Parent Liaison:
  360-725-6075

Both services are free and provide support for parents walking the advocacy path in Washington State. Many states have similar programs. Specifically, the OSPI Parent Liaison provides information related to Special Education issues and helps parents with the research end of the process. Whereas, the Governor's Office program is a true advocacy service and will be able to work with you in conflict resolution between the district and you.

Meetings: Maintaining Focus

Just when you think it's over and you feel like you can start to relax, you only have a four-to-six week window of "let's see – let it unfold" time while the staff puts into action what you all agreed upon (or not). As your child's advocate, your ability to follow-up with the commitments is as important, or even more so, than the initial IEP or 504 plan negotiations.

As a Principal, I learned the hard way that accountability is one of the weakest elements of the public school system. Teachers and Administrators often say what they mean, but there are a number of reasons many struggle to walk the talk. Unfortunately, this presents a slippery slope. I know this is harsh and warrants criticism from those who have put their best foot forward as public educators but this is one of the hard truths I have learned on this path. So, as your child's advocate, you need to keep the process and the decisions made on everyone's radar by remaining vigilant.

As an advocate for over 17 years, I have witnessed both sides of the accountability coin but often, commitments and mutually agreed upon decisions fall off by the wayside if parents let it slide. And that's where I come in. After the initial IEP or 504 plan, my primary focus is to assure the original agreements continue to align well with the student's "present levels of performance" and success continues over time.

- **Section 504**: The standard accountability check-in period for a 504 is **once a year**, usually following the initial implementation dates, i.e., October 2015 would result in a meeting October 2016 or before. This is not an intense compliance issue if the team is slightly off the due date, because the Section 504 governing body, the Office of Civil Rights, is another understaffed federal agency with far too much on its platter. You can request meetings throughout the year as a follow-up or as issues or concerns arise.
    - Due to the flexible nature of the 504 plan process, there are no formal evaluations associated with the annual meetings or set-in stone guidelines for qualification or continued support. In fact, when you read the guidelines (provided in an earlier section) you will see statements highlighting "broadly" in terms of qualification. However, it still is a matter of creating mutual understanding by connecting the dots via the disability, present levels of performance, and a perceived significant impact.
    - If your child's success on the 504 plan appears to diminish or plateau, following the initial four-to-six week period, or at any time during the 12 months in between meetings, requesting an evaluation for an IEP would be appropriate. Also, many students who receive support of a 504 in elementary school often need a more comprehensive level of support in the middle school; this is most evident with ADD/ADHD or Autism Spectrum students who are pushed over the edge with class schedules, additional homework requirements, and the intensity of adolescent social conditions. So an IEP would be most appropriate in many cases where 504 support is not making the grade.

- **IEP (Specially Designed Instruction):** The standard accountability check-in period is **once a year**, usually following the initial implementation dates, i.e., October 31, 2015 would result in a meeting prior to October 31, 2016. This is the annual meeting and needs to be completed prior to the compliance due date.

  - Schedule the annual IEP Review a month in advance of the scheduled due date (as well as the Three Year Evaluation).
  - Schools worry about meeting their due dates and often push things to the edge without providing ample time to forge a consensus based process. So, it's best to request the annual meeting (or three-year review) a month out from the actual compliance due date to allow breathing room if needed.

  - Annual meeting fundamentals include:
    a. Update the present levels of performance, including new evaluations, by asking the question: "What does learning currently look like for my child related to academic, behavior, communication-language, social-emotional, physical, and other considerations?" This should be evidence-based with data with opinions and subjective statements minimized as much as possible.
    b. Review and adjust the goals associated with specially designed instruction; they should be updated and moved forward with new learning targets each year. Specially, the team needs to address the question: "How effective was the specially designed instruction in review of annual goals?", "How was progress measured from the starting point of the current IEP in comparison to the present levels of performance?"
    c. Review and adjust the services, allocated minutes, and related accommodations as needed; **you can call a meeting anytime within reason**.
    d. Write all adjustments and modifications within the new IEP or 504 Plan and document within a PRIOR WRITTEN NOTICE.

- **Three-Year Evaluation - Review (IEP only):** This is a formal process, similar to the initial IEP, with the following steps conducted by expiration of the previous Evaluation:

  STEP ONE: As described in the initial IEP process, meet with your teachers, case manager, and support staff prior to meeting to understand their perspective before the Three-Year Evaluation process begins; know their agenda so you can prepare.

  STEP TWO: Pre-Evaluation Meeting: Opportunity to review the previous Evaluation, discuss progress, and determine what Evaluation assessments and tools will be required to complete the three-year update. The Evaluation will take no more than 35 school days from the date you signed permission to assess.

  STEP THREE: Evaluation Meeting: Opportunity to review the data and all the collected evidence pointing in the direction of continued eligibility or exiting from IEP services.

  - Eligible: connecting the dots between disability, present levels, and severity of disability on achievement; just like it was in the initial IEP. If a student continues to be eligible, a new IEP will be developed within 30 calendar days.

   o   Exiting: following a formal review of all evidence through an evaluation, your child
       is determined to not need specially designed instruction outside the General
       Education setting:
       a.   If the agenda is to "exit" your child against your wishes, see the section in the
            handbook, "If you do not agree with the decision".
       b.   If you do agree, immediately seek the support of 504 accommodations, so
            your child has appropriate support in the transition following the IEP.

Manifestation Hearing: And the Ten Day Grace Period (Disciplinary)

When a child with an identified disability through a 504 or an IEP engages in behavior or breaks a
school code of conduct and the school proposes to remove the child, the school must hold a hearing
to determine if the child's behavior was caused by his disability. This hearing, known as a
Manifestation Hearing, is a process to review the relationship between the child's disability and the
behavior, guided by the evidence presented. Evidence includes a review of:

- The suspension, expulsion, or other disciplinary documentation related to the incident
- The students Evaluation, IEP, and/or 504 Plan

Consequences for problem behaviors should not discriminate against a child based on his disability.
Though schools often suspend and expel students with disabilities for behavior caused by their
disabilities the following needs to be established:

- A Manifestation Hearing must be conducted within 10 days of a change of placement
  established by the proposal.
- Also, a Manifestation Hearing shall be conducted by the 10th day a student has been
  suspended from school whether it be in a row or within a cumulative ten days (as long as
  the behaviors of concerns are related)*

*   *When a student is removed from instruction, and sent to the office, and does not have access to
    the activities other students are provided, this is a suspension!*

The following questions guide this discussion:

- Was the behavior caused by or directly and substantially related to your child's disability?
- Was the behavior a direct result of the school's failure to implement your child's IEP?

"YES"   If one of the questions above were answered with "yes", then there is a manifestation
        between your child's behavior and disability. Remember, you are an equal participant at an
        IEP Team meeting! Be sure to explain why you think your child behaved inappropriately
        and how you think it is related to his or her disability.

When there is a manifestation, your child cannot be further disciplined. This means your child
cannot be recommended for expulsion or continue to be suspended for that behavior. Instead, the
IEP needs to be changed to address your child's behaviors. This often results in a Functional
Behavior Assessment (FBA) or an amendment to the current Behavior Intervention Plan (BIP).

"NO"   Then your son or daughter would be removed from school like any General Education
        student. However, Specially Designed Instruction via an IEP would need to be offered after
        ten days away from the instructional program.

Based upon my experience as a Principal as well as an Education Advocate, most disciplinary activity conducted by identified students, with a 504 Plan or an IEP, can be traced to an identified disability. This is most evident with students who experience the following:

- ADD/ADHD due to the nature of the diagnosis highlighted by Executive Functioning issues
- AUTISM related behaviors including anxiety, social language disorder, and hyper-focus.

ᘓ

Closing Comments

I cannot begin to tell you how often I hear from my clients the following: "The team responds differently when someone is working with me who knows the ropes." This can be even more apparent in matters related to a student's behavior, like Manifestation Hearing meetings, or other complex situations.

This is true, but the sole purpose of the "Insider's Guidebook" is to share tools and strategies I have acquired over the years to strengthen your advocacy position. Since you made it this far, you will also "know the ropes", and experience a difference in your relationship with staff and the overall intervention team. As a result, your child's 504 Plan or IEP will be more aligned with his or her needs. I can assure you this will happen! You will be taking control of your child's IEP and 504 Plan with confidence as long as you never lose focus on the following:

*The primary responsibility of an effective parent-advocate is to move the process from an emotionally charged conversation to an **evidence-driven approach**. By shifting the dialog with staff and teachers from subjective to **objective reasoning**, founded upon **mutual understanding**; you will gain control of your child's education plan and in the process, empower the team to strategically co-create the best IEP/504 plan possible for your child!*

I encourage to contact us when you are in need of more in-depth guidance at larrydavis@specialeducationadvocacy.org. or by phone, (888) 851-5905 / (206) 914-0975. It's our pleasure working with you for the path of education advocacy is an important one like no other.

Within this process, our goal is to ultimately allow the gifts within our children to unfold; and by doing so, we are making the world a better place one child at a time.

Blessings to you and yours.

Larry

APPENDIX: IEP & SECTION 504 PLAN FLOW CHART

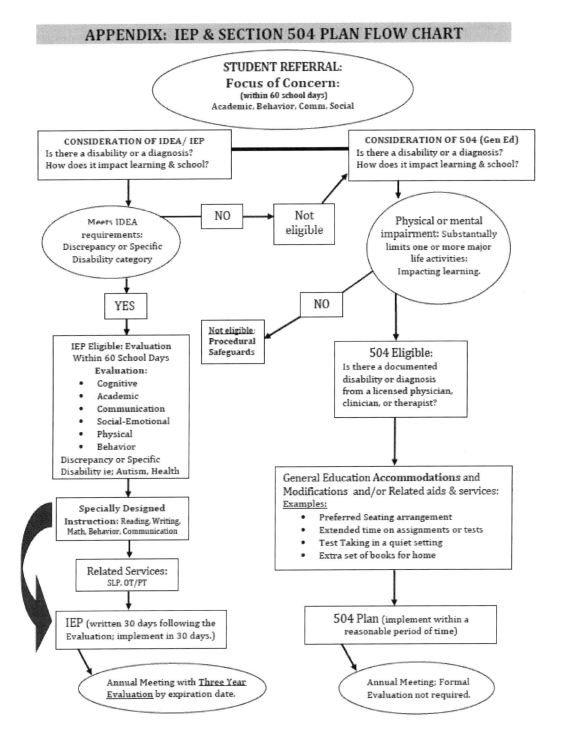

STUDENT REFERRAL:
Focus of Concern:
(within 60 school days)
Academic, Behavior, Comm, Social

CONSIDERATION OF IDEA/ IEP
Is there a disability or a diagnosis?
How does it impact learning & school?

CONSIDERATION OF 504 (Gen Ed)
Is there a disability or a diagnosis?
How does it impact learning & school?

Meets IDEA requirements: Discrepancy or Specific Disability category

NO → Not eligible

Physical or mental impairment: Substantially limits one or more major life activities: Impacting learning.

YES

NO

Not eligible: Procedural Safeguards

IEP Eligible: Evaluation Within 60 School Days
Evaluation:
- Cognitive
- Academic
- Communication
- Social-Emotional
- Physical
- Behavior

Discrepancy or Specific Disability ie; Autism, Health

504 Eligible:
Is there a documented disability or diagnosis from a licensed physician, clinician, or therapist?

Specially Designed Instruction: Reading, Writing, Math, Behavior, Communication

Related Services:
SLP, OT/PT

General Education **Accommodations** and Modifications and/or Related aids & services:
Examples:
- Preferred Seating arrangement
- Extended time on assignments or tests
- Test Taking in a quiet setting
- Extra set of books for home

IEP (written 30 days following the Evaluation; implement in 30 days.)

504 Plan (implement within a reasonable period of time)

Annual Meeting with Three Year Evaluation by expiration date.

Annual Meeting; Formal Evaluation not required.

About The Author: Larry Martin Davis

As a nationally recognized Educational Consultant & Advocate since 1998, Larry provides essential support to parents navigating the school system. Through direct IEP & 504 Plan advocacy and consulting in complex special needs casework, his practice **Special Education Advocacy.org** is considered one of the leading advocacy resources in the country, with expertise in Special Education and Gifted Education. In addition, Larry is a well-respected speaker at conferences across the country, including the annual NAESP Principals Convention, Autism Society, and SENG [Gifted Education] Annual Conferences.

In 2009, he was a recipient of the Puget Sound Super Hero Award presented by "Parent Map Magazine" due to his nationally recognized advocacy practice. Also, in 2014, "West Sound Home and Garden Magazine" acknowledged Larry as a "Local Hero". Insightful, intuitive, and graced with a quirky sense of humor: Simply, he serves parents and districts as a valued resource when addressing special needs intervention, gifted education programming, and highly complicated IEP and 504 Plan development.

Initially, Larry's career started as an Elementary Teacher in 1980. By the time he was 30, he was one of the youngest principals in California and loved being a school administrator for ten years. In the process of following his dream, being a school administrator, he discovered a new calling within Special Education, and developed his own advocacy practice in 1998. Author of two books; his most recent, "Love, Understanding, And Other Best Practices", is available through his website (www.specialeducationadvocacy.org), Amazon, CreateSpace Estore, and at online book sellers. Also, Larry joined the Institute of HeartMath program in April of 2011 and became certified as a Trainer offering workshops and presentations in support of emotional wellness, resiliency, and self-regulation; all critical issues within ADHD, Autism, and other anxiety related conditions.

As a nationally recognized speaker and trainer on various special education and gifted education topics, his audience consistently reviews his presentations as "inspiring", "informative", and "uplifting". The foundation of his work is guided by the belief that <u>**every child is a gift**</u> **and our role through advocacy is to assure the unfolding of the promise, possibility, and passion found within our children**.

Larry can be contacted directly at larrydavis@specialeducationadvocacy.org or by phone: (888) 881-5904 / (206) 914-0975.

Love, Understanding, and Other Best Practices:

The New School of Thought on IEP and 504 Plans

By Larry Martin Davis

Written for educators and parents; "Love, Understanding, and Other Best Practices", inspires a new paradigm in Special Education based upon *mutual understanding*. By engaging in authentic conversation across the table, highlighted by genuine partnership, and an evidence-based decision model, one of the most important opportunities to make a difference in a child's life will unfold. Within an inspired and insightful perspective, guided by "What works?", both IEP and 504 Plans support intervention based upon purpose, promise, and possibility. Though a quick read, this valuable resource guide presents transformative insights through personal stories leading toward creativity, innovation, and collaboration. This is so important for the traditional IEP and 504 intervention process has been described as "adversarial" and "us versus them". It's time for a shift to a new paradigm!

Taking Advocacy to Heart!

"Love, Understanding, and Other Best Practices" is **available now** through Amazon.com, CreateSpace eStore, Bookstores and Online Retailers:
You can visit us at Special Education Advocacy.org as well.